REOPENING
THE BACK DOOR

This book is great! It breaks open an issue in the life of the church that has been ignored and left to the wolves!

The Rev. James A. Rea
First Presbyterian Church
Salem, Oregon

I will have copies available in the church library and other places for general circulation.

The Rev. Robert Mushrush
First United Methodist Church
Rock Island, Illinois

Thoroughly biblical, sensible, applicable, motivational, and easy to understand.

Keith Dirks
Trinity Lutheran Church
Lincoln, Nebraska

A practical manual for convincing Christians of the urgency to reach out to inactive members and [then] showing them ways to do it.

Dr. Joseph I. Mortensen
First Baptist Church
Midland, Michigan

It is excellent. A book for all to read.

Fr. Thomas C. Petronek
St. Joseph's Catholic Parish
Tiltonsville, Ohio

The inactive member is a forgotten person in many congregations. Those who think about them find feelings of guilt, remorse, and anger. Thanks to this book we have new ways of dealing with these forgotten, yet important people.

The Rev. Ronald Martinson
Central Lutheran Church
Anchorage, Alaska

REOPENING
THE BACK DOOR

ANSWERS TO QUESTIONS ABOUT MINISTERING TO INACTIVE MEMBERS

KENNETH C. HAUGK

Tebunah Ministries
St. Louis • Missouri

Other books by Kenneth C. Haugk:

Christian Caregiving—a Way of Life

Antagonists in the Church: How to Identify and Deal with Destructive Conflict

The Quest for Quality Caring

Caring for Inactive Members: How to Make God's House a Home (Leader's Guide and Participant Manual for a 6-hour course)

Speaking the Truth in Love: How to Be an Assertive Christian (with Ruth N. Koch)

Discovering God's Vision for Your Life: You and Your Spiritual Gifts (Integrated set of resources for an 8-hour course)

Reopening the Back Door: Answers to Questions about Ministering to Inactive Members

Copyright © 1989, 1992 by Kenneth C. Haugk

You can secure information on the in-congregation training course *Caring for Inactive Members: How to Make God's House a Home,* of which *Reopening the Back Door* is the text, by writing Tebunah Ministries at the address above.

All Scripture quotations, unless otherwise noted, are from the New Revised Standard Version of the Bible, copyright © 1989 by the Division of Christian Education of the National Council of Churches of Christ in the United States of America.

ISBN: 0-9634093-0-1
Library of Congress Catalog Card Number: 92-096989

Printed in the United States of America

7 6 5 4 3 2
13 11 09 07 05 03

To caring Christians everywhere
who are concerned about
church inactivity,
and to inactive members everywhere
who struggle with their
pain and loss.

Contents

Preface

Over the years it has been my privilege to give hundreds of lectures and workshops on the topic of church inactivity. The interest on these occasions has been so great—matching my own intense concern—that both clergy and lay participants have barraged me with numerous questions before, during, and afterward. Frequently I asked that they submit these questions in writing, and they did—by the thousands! I have sifted through those thousands, looking for the most common as well as those to which the answers would be most illuminating.

The result is the 220 questions that make up this book, which my prayers and hopes earnestly desire to be a blessing for the church, for inactive members, and for the world that hungers for the ministry of all the people of God. I would like to see church involvement increase dramatically, and I know the approach espoused here is the one most likely to bring about that happy result.

In *Reopening the Back Door* one of my goals is to be personal. I want to reflect the pain, pathos, and needs of those who have been inactive. Additionally I seek to address the feelings—both pleasure and frustration—of those active members who have been relating to inactive members.

Another of my goals is be positive, which is essential because the subject of church inactivity has acquired an undeserved negative reputation. I know for a fact that both the church and its members can do much to address the issue of church inactivity successfully, with compassion and care. My experience and the experiences of many others bear me out: There is every reason to be positive.

This is an area of hope for the church!

Reopening the Back Door stands on its own as a resource for church staff, for lay leaders—actually, for every member of a congregation. The church has great needs when it comes to dealing with church inactivity, and every member can be a partner in addressing those needs. Reading this book by itself will suggest hundreds of ideas to the ones who take this problem seriously.

This book also serves a vital role as a textbook for the course entitled *CARING FOR INACTIVE MEMBERS: How to Make God's House a Home.* Within these covers you who are participants in that course will find anticipated many—perhaps most—of the questions that occur to you. You will also discover reinforcement for what you learn in the course and important new information to reflect on.

This book would never have come to be without the earnest willingness of the thousands of questioners who searched their hearts and openly shared with me what they found there. In addition, I gratefully acknowledge the more than 700 individuals from 20 denominations who contributed to manuscript review and revision through cycle after cycle of refinement. My thanks to you, one and all.

1

A New Beginning

The time has come to make a new beginning. Concern about church inactivity certainly weighs on the minds of Christians. Urgent concern for inactive persons themselves presses forth from Christian hearts. And out of these real concerns a clamor of questions emerges: Where can we as individuals begin? What can congregations do? What do we need to know?

Individuals and congregations can do much about church inactivity. And that's good, because there is much to do. Studies reveal that an average of approximately 30-35% of the membership of a congregation is inactive. These are hurting, homeless people. Concern for inactive members goes right back to Jesus' concern for people in need.

Just think of the potential for your church if a portion of those individuals should return to active participation. More than that, suppose you were able to prevent inactivity among currently active members! This is a factor often grossly ignored in the area of church growth—a second way to achieve that goal. (The first way is to gain new members.) I'm talking about retaining current members. Many churches have been practicing the principle of "two in the front door, one out the back door." Worse, some churches have experienced one in the front door, one out the back; and worst of all, some churches practice one in the front door, two out the back door.

Your new beginning involves some carpentry, not a bad trade for a people whose God became incarnate as a carpenter's son, who probably practiced carpentry himself before he began the tumultuous ministry of his last three years. What you need to do—and this book will teach you how to do—is work on that back door of your church, so it swings both ways.

Whoever you are, whatever place you occupy in your congregation, you can make a difference. You can prevent inactivity. You can relate caringly to inactive members. You can welcome them home should they decide to return.

Coming back is itself a project. It takes time. You can make homecoming worthwhile. When you take a proper approach to inactivity, you will participate in great wonders of reconciliation and healing. Just keep in mind, as you embark on this part of your spiritual journey, that reconciliation is a door that swings both ways. None of us has any credible claim to perfection or wholeness except as God made us so through an initiative that belongs wholly on God's side. It is in Christ that we are made whole, and we are all in Christ—active members and inactive members alike in a common journey of faith.

Great events can happen in a congregation that takes seriously the quality of its ministry to all its members. Happily, such a congregation is on a course that is also the best way to gain members. Retaining and gaining go hand in hand.

Great wonders can happen, and they begin with education and training. The "proper approach" I mentioned has not often been the practice when the church has concerned itself with inactive members. To the contrary, congregations have not dealt all that effectively with church inactivity precisely because they have used improper approaches, fueled primarily by anger and pain. They have made exactly the wrong moves, reached out in exactly the wrong ways. They have slammed the back door on the heels of the departing individuals. You are going to reopen the back door of your church to permit free access from all approaches, not just the front.

This book can change your approach from improper to

proper if you allow it to touch your attitudes and your actions. Individuals and congregations can perform no more caring act than that of learning how to better relate to inactive members. The more there are who sensitively understand and can act in caring, loving, and appropriate ways, the better for all.

Understanding is a start, but by no means the finish. I have always had a bias for the practical, a bias very evident here in *Reopening the Back Door.* Most of the questioners who pushed me for answers were not interested in airy speculation, but in getting to the heart of the matter. The tenor of many questions is along these lines: What do I do in this specific situation? What do I say? How can I reach out? What should I not do?

Learning to meet your fellow Christian's needs with compassion and caring will prove to be a joy. Contrary to most people's expectations, dealing with church inactivity is an exciting venture. You will experience joy rather than drudgery, warm certainty that you are being Christ's ambassador rather than being the church's hammer-dropper.

So here you are, ready to make a fresh start. You are about to develop understanding, learn practical skills, peek into the hearts of inactive and active members alike, and discover the joy of reaching out. As President John F. Kennedy said in his inaugural address:

> All this will not be finished in the first one hundred days. Nor will it be finished in the first one thousand days. . . . But let us begin.

2

Defining Church Inactivity

"In the beginning was the Word," the apostle John says. God turns out to be a definer, and a pretty good one at that (to no one's surprise). "You want to know what I've meant all these eons? Very well." And God speaks the Word made flesh. God utters *Jesus!* "This is what I mean," says God.

Human beings are definers, too, again no surprise. Created as we are in God's image, it is an entirely likely turn of events that we should start at the same beginning in the same way.

Q. How do you define *inactive members?*

A. Here is the definition of *inactive members* I like to work with:

> Inactive members are individuals who have chosen not to participate in the worship life, financial support, and program activities of the congregation.

Basically, individuals become inactive at the point where they begin to detach emotionally and physically from the congregation. This may mean reduced attendance or continued absence from worship services; it may mean reduced giving, or no giving; it may mean a reduction or stoppage of participation in church program activities.

Q. How do you distinguish between *inactive* and *unable?*

A. The criterion is freedom of choice. The inactive person chooses not to be involved; the unable person has no choice in the matter.

There can be many factors that deny choice. A person might be physically limited in mobility because of age or other disablement. But emotional incapacity is a very real fact of life, too. People with phobias or panic disorders, for example, are just as much without choice as the person who is bedridden. One estimate suggests that as much as 5% of the population suffers from phobias of one kind or another. One type of phobia, agoraphobia, defined as fear of open spaces, shows itself in several ways. Agoraphobics are afraid of being trapped in public places from which they would be unable to escape without embarrassment if they should experience a panic attack. Victims of this irrational dread may not be able to drive across bridges, and if the only way to get to church is to cross a bridge, they can't do it.

People who have such emotional struggles are likely to be very private people because they experience shame about their situation. They are leery of talking with people who won't understand how they can be totally incapacitated by a circumstance or exposure that is utterly mundane to everyone else. Your ministry to these people is different, but starts from the same basis of compassionate understanding you need with inactive members: Have a heart.

Those who are separated from church by distance—because they are serving in the military, for example, or attending college in another city—are likewise obviously unable to attend their home congregation. So is the person whose job requires being out-of-town during the worship time.

By contrast, the inactive person could come, but chooses

not to. You will find out very quickly in talking to an individual which category he or she belongs to.

Q. How long should a person be gone from the congregation to be considered inactive?

A. Length of time is not the main criterion. In fact, a person might not be "gone" at all, and yet still be someone at risk. The chief factor to look at is whether the person is emotionally *moving away* from the congregation, starting to pluck out the life supports. An individual could conceivably be gone for weeks or even months, and yet if there is a good reason for that, if the person still feels a part of the congregation, inactivity is not the issue. On the other hand, a person could theoretically be gone only one week and yet be one who is emotionally separating from the congregation. That latter individual is either inactive or in the process of becoming inactive. Special keenness to early signs is vital. A person might be in attendance every Sunday and yet be what I call "pre-inactive."

Q. You mention choosing not to take part in worship, financial support, and programs as the criteria. But there are a number of people in our congregation who worship regularly and are pretty consistent in their giving, and that's it. They might take part in a few special functions. Are they inactive?

A. No, I would not consider them inactive. In some ways, you could argue that anyone who isn't spending 20-30 hours a week in church-related affairs is inactive. That is not what I mean, however, when I use the term. One individual with whom I shared this question said:

> I would have been overjoyed if my father had chosen the level of church involvement described in this question.

If a person is participating in all three areas—worship, financial support, and programs—however minimally, I would prefer to speak of "levels of activity" rather than inactivity. Probably it would be better for these individuals to be more involved—they are people still on the threshold of God's home—but at least they are involved.

Q. Isn't the term *inactive member* quite negative?

Q. Is there a better term to use than *inactive member?*

A. You might like the term better after you've had a chance to hear some of the alternatives. These are some of the terms in actual use that I've encountered:

Absentees
Apostates
Back door Christians
Backsliders
Black sheep Christians
Bystanders
C and E's (Christmas and Easter attenders)
Casual attenders
Casual Christians
Deadwood
Delinquent Christians (or just Delinquents)
Disaffiliates
Estranged church members
Fallen-away brethren
Fringe members
Lapsed members
Marginal members
Parish dropouts (or Dropouts)
Slippers
Suspended animation
Wayward Christians

The problem with most of these terms for me is the offensive connotations they carry. They are basically judgmental rather than descriptive. *Inactive member* is much better because it is descriptive. It refers to people's activity level, not their character.

Think of it from the point of view of the inactive member for a moment. Can you imagine such a person saying, "Last year I was a *lapsed* member"? Or how about, "I was a *delinquent* for six years"? I can't.

Inactive member is the term that many people who are or have been inactive actually choose when they refer to themselves and their church involvement. They don't cringe when they hear that term. Here is what one formerly inactive member said:

> I like the phrase *inactive member* because it's just matter-of-fact. It doesn't sound like a put-down or an insult directed at me because of my past status. Neither does it make me feel like I have to defend the inactive people I presently know and love when I hear the phrase used.

I'm always ready to use a more precise term in place of a less precise one, but short of reciting "not-currently-participating-in-worship-giving-and-programming" every time the need arises, the term *inactive member* seems to be the most caring one to use. By the way, this is not to say that you should use this terminology when you are talking with inactive members. If the subject comes up that they haven't been worshipping for a while, or haven't been taking part in programs, then those would be the words you would use, not *inactive*. You would not be relating to an "inactive member," but to a person with a name!

Q. Why do members suddenly become inactive?

A. It may look as if they "suddenly" become inactive, but in the vast majority of instances there is nothing sudden about it. Typically the final movement away from the church completes a long-term process with multiple causes at work.

For those individuals who do suddenly become inactive, and there are some, the cause most often relates to a crisis in their lives—internal or external. An internal crisis may be some emotional tidal wave that snaps all the moorings one had. An external crisis may be a family upheaval, for instance, that saps one's energies for anything but survival. Even in instances of crisis, however, individuals are more likely to become inactive if there are other causes at work.

Q. What are the biggest misconceptions people have about inactive members?

A. There is a whole collection of misconceptions, most having to do with prejudging what goes on inside inactive members:

1. "They" are all lazy.
2. "They" have lost their faith.
3. "They" are all apathetic.
4. "They" don't want to come back.
5. "They" want to be left alone.
6. "They" will come back on their own.
7. "They" will come back if you bully them.
8. "They" only need to be reminded of duty.
9. "They" will come back after a brief telephone call.
10. "They" need to be told what to do.
11. "We" don't have to deal with their feelings or try to understand them.
12. Whatever the problem, it's "their" responsibility, not "ours."

Every one of these assumptions is hasty and presumptuous. A lot of listening and care has to be invested first, before any assessments can be made. Certainly, there are some inactive members whose faith has weakened. (There are also some active members whose faith has weakened.) Sure, there are some inactive members who have become apathetic, or want to be left alone. There may even be a few who are genuinely lazy. For the vast majority, however, each situation will prove to be much different than any or all these misconceptions put together. Your job is to find out how the situation differs and then to be the most compassionate, caring person you can be.

Q. How do you discover who inactive persons are?

A. One person I shared this question with said:

This question really surprises me. It never occurred to me that congregations would have any difficulty with this. In our congregation we just look on the membership list, and whoever's not in church, that's the list of inactive members. But I can see how in larger congregations where people may not be known so well, it could be more complicated than that.

Well, it is and it isn't. First of all, the question has behind it a deeper one, which is, "How do we detect inactivity in the earliest stages?" And secondly, even small congregations would benefit by some forms of organization that would ensure that no one slips through the cracks. All that said, here are some practical ways to discover who inactive members are:

1. Pastors and other church staff can note who is and who is not attending. (The pastor of one church I know always checked off attendance against a membership list even before he disrobed, while it was still fresh in his mind.)

2. One or more leadership groups can occasionally go over the membership list, pooling their corporate awareness to determine who might be inactive.

3. Denominations that have frequent communion along with registration cards for communion have a very convenient means of "taking attendance."

4. For pledging members, the pattern of their contributions may change. Those who record and deposit contributions might pass along their observations of these changes to the appropriate individuals—the pastor or members of an inactive member ministry team. Please note, however, that a decrease or a cessation of giving should never be the subject matter of a visit, though it may be what prompts a visit. (See the question and answer on pages 181-182.) That is, don't go to the possibly inactive member and say, "We

noticed your contributions are down. What's up?" No matter how you phrase it, the person is going to be convinced you're only interested in the church finances.

5. Some congregations have instituted a "rite of friendship" that includes passing a sign-up sheet up and down the pews. This can be an excellent way of determining changes in patterns of attendance.

6. Some churches have shepherding/deacon/zone plan programs where certain members are designated to keep in touch with other members.

7. Through listening to people themselves, really listening to them, you can pick up many indicators of early inactivity.

8. The grapevine can be a source of leads on people who might be in the early stages of inactivity. Especially keep a preventive eye on those who are undergoing various life crises. They are prime candidates for inactivity.

9. Computers can help you keep track of important information. Statistical programs that will help you identify changes in patterns for individuals are among the most valuable you can have in your computer. Your output might be lists of those whose patterns of attendance or contributions have changed. And by the way, for churches in the computer age, those knowledgeable individuals who are willing to volunteer time for data entry are to be treasured as much as bookkeepers and counters.

All these nine suggestions are ways to gather data. None of them is any guarantee that the data, once gathered, will be used. Data is useless until it has been turned into information, which is data rendered intelligible to a human being. Don't just gather data for its own sake, but allow it to guide and direct you to begin ministry and outreach efforts.

Q. I could imagine approaching someone as inactive and having the person be insulted by the suggestion. Isn't it normal for people to wax and wane in their enthusiasm? Or is that a failure of the church?

A. You don't have to be absolutely sure someone is definitely inactive, or heading in that direction, in order to approach him or her, because you are not going to start your conversation by saying, "So, you're not that interested in church anymore, eh?" Instead, in all likelihood you will start with a simple question: "How are things going with you?" Generally no one objects to being sought out with caring concern, so your attention will be appreciated, not scorned.

Fluctuations in members' involvement is normal. To have 100% of the people in a church 100% eager to be involved in the ministry and programs of the church 100% of the time—this would be a very pleasant state of affairs for church leaders and staff to face. Unreal, but pleasant.

The reality in congregations is different. People do wax and wane in their availability for involvement and service, and that's okay. People's lives change. They start new jobs, go to school, have children, retire. Some of these changes will influence people to be more or less involved with the church.

Of course, everyone should continue to grow spiritually, should be stimulated and encouraged in love of the Lord, and should deepen relationship with God. *Shoulds* are terrible motivators, however. Where the church needs to upgrade its capabilities is in helping people see how their health and well-being depend on a continued deepening of their relationship with God. This is not necessarily a failure of the church, but just a part of the continuing challenge the church faces.

One way churches can better meet this challenge is by speaking the truth of the Gospel, the "for-you-ness" of the Gospel, in loud and clear tones. God's love is a love meant *for you.* Jesus Christ died *for you.* Another important part of God's plan for the structure of the church is the priesthood of all believers. When every Christian sees him- or herself as a minister with a sacred trust, and holy gifts to enable that trust, we will be much closer to the 100% dream I started out by sharing.

3

Moving from the Negative to the Positive

A friend of mine was an intrigued participant in a conversation with church friends. They were discussing what to do about inactivity and how to relate to inactive members. My friend had been describing the many reasons people become inactive.

"Personally, I couldn't relate well to inactive members. I'm too angry at them," said a strongly committed Christian woman.

A man spoke hesitantly: "A lot of what you say about inactive members' reasons for not attending may be true for some, but others are just making excuses."

My friend ventured to remark that inactive members often offer excuses initially, but as one gets to know them, they let one in on the real reasons.

He could tell, however, that the two individuals felt he was trying to talk them out of certainties on their part, so they passed to other topics with my friend wiser for the exchange. He had a fresh appreciation for the way negative feelings and misconceptions can interfere with motivation to care for inactive members.

Motivation is a word to which many a book has been devoted, and yet still it is a misunderstood term in common parlance.

Many think that motivation is all about "Making people want to do" thus-and-so. It is not. The unvarnished fact, a stumbling block to many a parent and many a dictator, is that no one can *make* anyone want to do anything. Motivation is always internally generated, never externally imposed.

You can make people do something, which is not at all the same as making them want to do it. This kind of "motivation" is usually coupled with some form of threatened punishment or denial: "Jones, you'll get here on time or be fired!" and "No dessert until you eat your brussels sprouts." The actual, internal motivation for the individual may be fear, preservation of security, or the desire for some good that is only available after some bad has been swallowed.

Since motivation is always internally generated, what can churches and individuals do to tie in to those internal needs and wants? That is the substance, in one way or another, of the questions in this chapter.

Q. How do you motivate the general congregation to be concerned about inactivity?

A. The bad news is, you can't. The good news is, you don't have to! At least in terms of a basic concern, the initial motivation is already present in large degree for many active members. Nearly all Christians have persons they know and care about who are inactive—friends, family members, people to whom they are very close. Some do have negative feelings toward *inactive members* when that term is used generally, but when they begin to personalize it, they make the connection that such-and-so an inactive member is really Mary, Joe, and their neighbor next door. At that point, the innate compassion Christians have for one another is released.

I have seen this repeatedly in workshops I have conducted on the topic. I am continually—and pleasantly—surprised to discover that those in attendance who are ordinary members, ones with no particular leadership role in the church, exhibit a great concern for inactive members.

Q. How can I help active members become more aware of their part in ministry to inactive members?

A. Now this is a different question from the one just prior, and it is one that congregations and individuals can do something about. The answer comes in the form of education and training. The first form this might take is in raising people's understanding of just what the "priesthood of all believers" really means. As members' awareness of and responsibility for their own ministry role is awakened and elevated, their response in ministry to inactive members will likewise heighten.

Q. Why are so many active members unwilling to visit inactives?

Q. Why are so many active members afraid even to relate casually to inactive members?

A. There can be all kinds of fears operating in an active person's mind: fear of rejection, of being exposed to anger, of uncertainty, of doing something new, of the amount of time it might take. This is also a case where a little bit of knowledge can be dangerous. By that I mean an active member might have been sensitized to the fact that there are right ways and wrong ways to communicate with an inactive member, without knowing what those right and wrong ways are. The active member gets "frozen up" lest he or she say the wrong thing.

Some people just see themselves as shy, not very good at social skills. "I can't make small talk," they say. This is good news, because "small talk" is not what an inactive member needs! "Large *listening*" is what an inactive member needs, and anyone can learn to do that.

Informal or casual relating, in a chance encounter on the street, say, is different. There is often an unspoken assumption that in any meeting with an inactive member you have to bring up the subject of church, but this is not the case. Far better just to greet them warmly and express your natural pleasure at seeing them again. Be your natural, friendly self. Don't berate—relate!

Another area of resistance is connected with what the goals of visiting or relating are and what they ought to be. If goals are established as "getting the inactive person back to church at all costs," this violates the active members' sense of themselves as caring Christians, yet too often such goals—*results goals,* I call them—are exactly the presumed goals a congregation establishes. Perhaps a few people are naturally comfortable with the hard-sell, high-pressure approach, but the great majority of people are not—nor should they be! If the goals are instead those of establishing a relationship and determining the inactive member's needs, then discomfort will diminish, maybe even vanish. Such positive goals, which I call *process goals,* fit very naturally into people's ideas of what ministry really ought to be.

Q. I thought a hard-line approach was called for—you know, "Be active or else!" Are you telling me that's not the way to do it?

A. If you communicate "Be active or else" to an inactive person, he or she will certainly choose "else." Unfortunately, the hard-line approach is the one often taken, and everyone loses. Relating to people with a results approach sets up a lose-lose situation. A process approach is essentially a win-win situation.

Q. Tell me more about results goals and process goals. What are they?

A. Active members often make the mistake of thinking that the main goal of relating to inactive members is to get them to come back to church, or to change their views, or to get them to forgive and forget. These are all results goals. In effect, the active member has decided ahead of time what is best for all concerned, and that outcome therefore is what he or she strives for.

This is playing God with someone else's life.

Results goals and process goals differ in focus. In the chart on the next page I have summarized these differences.

When the Caring Person Focuses on Results Goals	When the Caring Person Focuses on Process Goals
The emphasis is on outcomes.	The emphasis is on fundamentals, the building blocks of relating, e.g., listening, loving, caring.
Curing is the aim.	Caring is the aim.
The caring person feels responsible for results.	Results belong to God and the care receiver.
Focus is on the future.	Focus is on the present.
Pressure is increased on both the caring person and the one receiving care.	Pressure is lifted from the caring person and the one receiving care.
The Law becomes seductive.	The Gospel is operating.
Trust and faith reside in the caring person, who is seen as the agent for change.	Trust and faith reside in God, and God will use the process to bring about change.
The caring person focuses on what the one receiving care does or does not do.	The caring person focuses on what he or she is doing in the caring relationship.
The caring person is responsible for the one receiving care.	The caring person is responsible for him- or herself.
Growth and change are stymied.	Growth and change occur.

Process goals focus on the needs of the inactive member. The goals you establish are listening to the other, caring for the other, sharing Christian love with the other, and encouraging the other. A process approach empowers the other individual, rather than stripping away personhood and autonomy.

This is being a Christian servant.

Mind you, there is nothing wrong with results—far from it! There is nothing wrong with having inactive members come back to church. There's nothing wrong with having them forgive, or with our forgiving them. There's nothing wrong with barriers going down and attitudes changing—everyone's attitudes. There's nothing wrong, except that when you push for results, results flee.

Q. What is the best way to help lay people get over their fear of reaching out to inactive members?

A. Training and practice: Fear dissolves when people have learned they can be adept, not inept, at relating to inactive members. Education helps by showing that inactive members are "just folks" like you and me. When the myths about inactive members are dispelled—that they are lazy, or self-satisfied, or unbelieving—active members are freed to see them as people with hurts and problems and needs for ministry. A whole new attitude of outreach becomes possible then.

There is nothing like education and training to improve self-confidence, and there is nothing like improved self-confidence for evaporating fear.

Q. I would feel embarrassed approaching an inactive member. How can I get over that embarrassment?

A. Some people are just shy, and feel embarrassed about approaching others. The great discovery is that others will think you a fascinating conversationalist if you just learn to ask good questions and let them do most of the talking. This also happens to be the key in relating to inactive members. Let them do the bulk of the talking.

Maybe you also need to ask yourself why you are approaching an inactive member. Many times individuals feel embarrassed at that prospect because their motivation is wrapped around the fixed idea that the purpose of talking to inactive members is to get them to change, or to get them back in church. This kind of results orientation is bound to make you feel guilty and embarrassed. The antidote in this instance is to keep telling yourself that you are simply relating because you care.

Q. How do I overcome my anger toward inactive members?

A. Given half a chance, active members can easily build up a list of resentments against inactive members. "They get to sleep in." "They don't have to do all these duty things I do to support the church." "They must have piles of excess money because they sure aren't contributing to the church." "They are letting down the church I love!"

Overcoming these feelings will not necessarily happen very easily, but the place to start is with forgiveness. Forgiving whom? Yourself. You don't forgive you, of course. God forgives you. You need to recognize that you are in need of forgiveness, too, and ask for it. You too are a sinner and in need of God's grace and love.

Don't set about relating to inactive members formally or informally until you have straightened out this problem of anger by offering it to God. Your anger will do nothing to help your relating to inactive members.

Education and training will help dispel anger, too. When correct information is available about inactive members, attitudes can change very rapidly. When you realize the hurts that they may have experienced in church, or the crises that may have occurred in their lives, your attitude of anger is likely to melt away in the warmth of your compassion.

Jesus is a good model to follow. How did he behave toward the woman at the well? Toward the two tax-collectors, Levi and

Zacchaeus? Toward the prostitute? It is our "good fortune," God's Good News, that he sees us the same way he saw them.

Q. In a concern to avoid judgmentalism, will I fail to maintain any standards whatever?

A. Some active members see inactivity as the operation of sin in the lives of inactive members—which it is—and go from that to seeing inactive members simply as sinners. This is self-defeating and deadly to ministry. To know that sin exists in the nature of another does not move your understanding forward any because sin operates in the nature of us all—expressing itself now in inactivity, now in lust, now in self-righteous behavior, and so on through the whole discount-store catalog. Furthermore, to classify inactive members merely as sinners actually sets you back substantially because then your attitude toward them is inevitably going to be judgmental and angry.

Your standards apply to you, not someone else. Just because an inactive member might have different views or behavior doesn't mean that you have to adopt those standards for yourself, or even endorse them.

By all means maintain your own standards. For example, I do not think you ought to skip church on Sunday for the purpose of visiting an inactive member—just because you expect that he or she will be home at that time!

In the process of caring for others you are being Jesus Christ to them, as high a standard as any human can strive to maintain, part of the rare partnership God has granted us as his children. Their spiritual growth doesn't depend on what you do for them, but what God does in them.

If you come across in a heavy-handed, legalistic way—"Ralph, I'm here to tell you what the will of the Lord is for you"—you may be in the unfortunate position of being right but not being helpful. Do you want to be right, or do you want Ralph to come back to church? (And yes, it's all right to want Ralph to come back to church. Just don't push for that result.) Remember, too, that you may not have heard the person's whole point yet, but simply the preface. That's why listening is so important.

When you relate to inactive members who hold particular positions with which you disagree, how you convey that fact makes a major difference. Are you calm and genuine about it, owning your own feelings and opinions very directly? Or do you throw a fit, casting the inactive person into outer darkness for being silly and in error? The first reaction promotes growth, the second stifles it.

Q. How about church leaders—elders, council members, deacons? How do you get them excited about ministry to inactive members?

A. The same solutions apply as you move up the ladder of church leadership. Elders, deacons, committee members—some may seem lethargic when it comes to fulfilling part of their role, if that role is described to include ministry to inactive members. But this apparent lethargy will likewise yield to skill training, to be replaced by competence and confidence.

Church leaders also have to get out of a results mode of thinking and into a process mode. People who relate to inactive members from a process point of view will get great pleasure, great joy from doing it. But neither church leaders nor ordinary folks get any pleasure out of thinking that they are being watched and measured to see what results they can show.

Every incoming elder's or other congregation leader's orientation should include a job description covering the tasks and time expected of him or her. Are the duties of their position commensurate with their gifts? Sometimes people are coerced into taking on certain roles of leadership (a danger sign for future inactivity!) without any attention given to whether the roles they are being asked to fill fit their gifts. Training will help here too, but matching gifts to ministry requirements is wise.

Q. Which spiritual gifts are particularly useful in ministry to inactive members?

A. In a congregation's overall approach to inactive members, here are the gifts that are important.

For those contacting inactive members

1. The gift (Rom. 12:8; Greek, *eleos*) typically translated as "mercy," which is better translated as "empathic caring"

2. The gift of service (Rom. 12:7, 1 Cor. 12:5; Greek, *diakonia*)

3. The gift of exhortation (Rom. 12:8; Greek, *paraklesis*), better understood as "encouragement" or "comfort"

For those leading the ministry to inactive members

4. The gift of leadership (Rom. 12:8; Greek, *proistemi*), better understood as "caring leadership" or "mother henning"

5. The gift of administration (1 Cor. 12:28; Greek, *kubernesis*), better translated as "governance"

6. The gift of teaching (Rom. 12:7, 1 Cor. 12:28, Eph. 4:11; Greek, *didaskalos*), because training of those reaching out to inactive members is so important

Elements of other gifts—wisdom, knowledge, faith, evangelism—come into play, too. The promise that the Apostle Paul makes to the church is sure: ". . . so you are not lacking in any spiritual gift as you wait for the revealing of our Lord Jesus Christ" (1 Cor. 1:7). This can be an encouragement to you and the church leaders as you consider establishing a true ministry approach to inactive members.

Q. What else could be said to motivate our congregational leadership?

A. Here are just a few points:

1. Inactivity is not unique to our congregation. Every congregation has this problem.

2. There are inactive people out there who are hurting. Our congregation would be well-advised to learn how to prevent inactivity and to relate to the ones who are already inactive as well as those who are becoming inactive.

3. When a congregation emphasizes overall ministry to inactive members, benefits flow to the whole congregation—the quality of ministry in the congregation is improved for both active and inactive members.

4. Inactive members should not be blamed; neither should congregations and leaders be blamed. What is important is to minister effectively.

5. Ministry to inactive members can be extremely successful—in many ways.

There may be someone in your congregation who was inactive once, has since returned, and is making a significant contribution to the church. Get the leadership thinking about how many other talented, gifted people might be out there. You might also note for the leaders the fact that, given X-Y-Z set of circumstances, anyone can become inactive—the leaders, or someone in their families, for instance. Encourage them to ask themselves how they would like to be treated if that were to happen, or how they would like the church to respond to someone in their families. This is the way to respond to existing inactive members now.

Q. What will help get pastors excited about being involved in inactive member ministry?

A. You'll be surprised how many pastors become excited when they start to realize others in the congregation are willing to take on some of the responsibility for this area of ministry! Traditionally the responsibility has fallen to them alone, with the church board casting a hard eye on their efforts, looking for results.

The premise that results were what counted has been common belief, as if it were beyond question.

Unfortunately, that attitude is just exactly backward. Here's a story from someone I know:

> One summer while in college I volunteered 10 weeks of my summer vacation as a Parish Worker. My pastor and I were both involved that summer calling on inactive and unchurched people. I was into the process and didn't feel particularly pressured about results. That fall, 26 people joined or rejoined the church.
>
> The next summer I was employed by the congregation as a Parish Worker. Since I was now being paid, I felt a great deal of pressure to produce results. I felt that it was up to me. The outcome of that summer was one inactive member who returned, but is now sporadic in attendance again, and no new church members at all. While the first summer had been a real joy because I'd simply concentrated on getting to know people and care for them, the next summer left me frustrated, feeling that I'd failed the congregation.

The emphasis I recommend—on process rather than results—will take one pressure off pastors. The fact of others' involvement will relieve another pressure, that of loneliness. Replacing these pressures will be the joy of working cooperatively in the training and equipping of people, in which the pastor's efforts will be invaluable.

When it comes to establishing and maintaining quality relationships, focusing on process goals is healthy. Focusing on results goals is not. You will need to have a healthy respect for how results-oriented most people's thinking is, probably including your own! It is much more difficult than you might think to teach—and learn—a process orientation. If the concept seems elusive to you, review this chapter several times.

4

Common Mistakes and How to Avoid Them

With a definition in hand, and a new view of motivation—now you might be ready and willing to get started doing something as an individual, as a congregation, anything to satisfy your natural Christian concern for the well-being of inactive members. Hold on there! First pay attention to some hazards and mistakes to avoid.

The first mistake to consider is one of attitude, and it is a product of our results-oriented society.

Q. Is there a streamlined approach to ministry to inactive members?

A. That would depend on what you mean by streamlined. If you mean, "Is there a quick and easy way to contact inactive members, lasso them, and drag them back to the corral?" the answer is no. As with any of the other quality activities of the church, there is no quick and easy way to do ministry.

Welcome to life this side of heaven.

If what you mean by streamlined, however, is the removal of attitudes and practices that hinder carefully planned, quality

39

ministry, then the answer is yes. The streamlined approach is a process-oriented approach as opposed to a results-oriented approach.

A results-oriented approach focuses on the future and on ends. It increases pressure on everyone, active and inactive members alike. A results-oriented approach to inactive member ministry futilely tries to take away from God and the inactive member outcomes that are theirs to achieve.

A process-oriented approach focuses on the present, and on means. It reduces pressure on both the inactive member and the active member. It leaves control with God and the inactive member, while leaving active members with control that properly belongs to them—that is, control of their own actions.

Q. Our congregation is thinking about starting a ministry program to inactive members. Before we do, we want to know: What percentage can we expect to come back to church?

A. Suppose the answer were *only 1 out of 100*—would you proceed? You would if you knew your Bible:

> "Which one of you, having a hundred sheep and losing one of them, does not leave the ninety-nine in the wilderness and go after the one that is lost until he finds it? When he has found it, he lays it on his shoulders and rejoices. And when he comes home, he calls together his friends and neighbors, saying to them, 'Rejoice with me, for I have found my sheep that was lost.'"
>
> Luke 15:4-6

Your question is valid, but only when it is not the *only* question you are asking. Needing guarantees ahead of time can sound the death-knell to ministry to inactive persons, or any kind of ministry for that matter. It can also come dangerously close to disclaiming God's authorship of the work of the church.

The actual response will be much higher than 1 in 100, and indeed, in one way it will be close to 100 out of 100! Ministry, relating with care, is never wasted in the good it does both for the one who is ministered to and the one who ministers.

Even if an inactive member doesn't come back to church, you will have ministered to that person while you were with him or her. The individual is more likely to be closer to God even though still inactive. You will have been one link in the chain of caring that God is forging for that person.

Furthermore, when you do minister to an inactive member, you're going to learn—about yourself, about the congregation, and about the quality of the congregation's response to its call to be a home for the people of God. What you learn will help you make the congregation stronger, which will decrease the likelihood of people becoming inactive in the future. This sort of multiplication of benefits is a mark of God's economy in action.

Just exactly what your numbers will look like depends on many factors. John Savage states that one congregation experienced an 86% return rate; another congregation experienced a 60% return rate.[1] One user of the course *CARING FOR INACTIVE MEMBERS: How to Make God's House a Home*[2] had this to say:

> We identified 120 inactive members on our membership list. In contacting them, we found that 60 had moved away or joined another congregation; 19 were in the military, away at college, or had another valid reason; *and 41 welcomed the call and follow-up contact.*

This is 100% results by anyone's definition!

And yet results are not what you focus on in ministry to inactive members. We minister to them because they are "ours." More to the point, "they are us" as the Body of Christ. We received them into active membership, and we assumed a Christian responsibility in so doing. It was a mutual commitment, and even though they might appear to be reneging on their side of the commitment, that is no excuse for us to renege on our responsibility.

Q. Can results-oriented people be satisfied with a process-oriented approach?

A. Once results-oriented people have been trained in a process-oriented approach, many will be more than satisfied—they will be ecstatic! People thrive on a process-oriented approach because it finally gives them permission to stop butting their heads against a wall when reaching out to inactive persons.

Some results-oriented people just may not have the temperament for this kind of ministry, however. That's all right, the church is a place for many gifts. Turn them loose on projects that do benefit from a results-oriented approach: decorating the sanctuary for Christmas, putting on a church supper, taking charge of a planned addition to your church facilities. (And even in these activities, I hope they will take a process-oriented approach as they relate to the people involved.)

Training ought not be limited just to those who seem to have a natural process bent, however. There aren't that many who naturally fit this description, for one thing. Process thinking is alien to most, but it most definitely can be learned. The results-oriented people in your congregation especially ought to be trained because otherwise they may be the loudest critical voices of inactive members. Somewhere along the line, without training, results-oriented persons will probably end up fracturing a relationship you have been carefully nurturing with an inactive member. To prevent this, train as many as possible in your congregation.

Q. What if you're in a situation where individuals visiting inactive members are judged on the basis of how successful they are in getting people back to church?

A. Who's doing that judging? Whoever it is probably doesn't know any better, and you have a golden opportunity to educate him or her. You will in any case be involved in a continuing education effort in your congregation to make sure that as many people as possible get relieved of that mistaken and fruitless notion.

False expectations could produce a serious problem, obviously, when they come from either the pastor of the congregation or the leader of a team that is calling on inactive members. The situation is likewise ripe for misunderstanding if there are individuals with mistaken expectations of the pastor. Education is still the key. For starters, give those individuals this book. Offer to explore some of Jesus' parables with them: The lost sheep (Luke 15:3-7); the lost coin (Luke 15:8-10); the prodigal son (Luke 15:11-32). Set up and conduct training courses, too.

Without being high and mighty about it, you would be well-advised to steer clear of a results-oriented outreach program to inactive members, in those rare instances where the person of influence remains unconvinced of the value of a process-oriented approach. Such a program will do more harm than good. This sounds tough, but don't worry about it. The virtues of a process-oriented approach are too readily apparent when anyone takes the time to explore the theology and ministry attitude that are its foundation. For the most part people will seize it with a glad cry.

Q. Our congregation sends a letter to those who have been inactive for three months. Three months after that we send a follow-up letter. This approach doesn't seem to be working too well. Either we get angry replies, or no replies at all. Is there something we should know about letter-writing?

A. There most certainly is—don't do it!

Sending letters exhorting inactive individuals to come back to church is one of the most practiced and least effective means of trying to reach them. It doesn't do any good, and it may very well put even more distance between inactive members and the church. In seminars I have sometimes asked, "Has anyone seen an instance when a letter to an inactive member brought someone back to church?" Once a participant said, "Yes, my family was inactive, and we received one of those letters. We got so angry, we decided to join another church!"

I know why congregations send them. It's a lot easier to send a letter than it is to make personal contact, which raises all sorts of possibilities for anxiety if the interaction is more than one is prepared for.

Q. But aren't such letters to people, or articles in newsletters, better than nothing?

A. No, they do more damage than good. They drive people away; they give people further reason to stay away.

In addition to being impersonal, another problem with letters and articles of this type is that they often are accusatory-sounding, and they will almost always be perceived that way whether intended so or not. A letter is very one-sided, and because it is, it can set up a superior-inferior undertone to the communication. Even when the letter invites the inactive person to respond, it comes across that the writer is interested in only one response, and that is to *get back to church*!

If your choice is between doing nothing or sending a letter, do nothing. You will do more ministry by doing less damage.

Q. What about just sending other pieces of material to inactive members, perhaps with a relationship-building note?

A. Maybe, as long as there's no hidden hook in what you send—remember, process, not results. The best way to feel clean about your motives is to send the same communications to everyone, or at least to many in the congregation, not just to inactive members. Some congregations routinely send birthday and anniversary cards to all members, for instance. If inactive members are being treated like everyone else, this is a plus.

Notes or letters in combination with personal contacts are certainly acceptable and appropriate, always presuming they are part of a continuing effort to build a relationship. By themselves, they are incomplete.

Q. How effective is a telephone ministry to inactive members?

A. As with encouraging notes and cards, telephone calls can be a good supplement but not a substitute for personal contact. There are limitations to how relational you can be over the phone, and it is the relationship that will make the difference. Here's what one individual said:

> In one sense I suppose a phone call is also personal contact, but it's not in-person contact, and the communication suffers from lack of opportunity to "read" the other's nonverbal cues. I think good process-oriented caring for inactives is in large part a matter of sensing and feeling one's way along. I find my sensitivity to the other much reduced when I am deprived of the visual cues to how the person is feeling.

An effective, quality ministry to inactive members that truly shares Christ's love must have face-to-face contact as its primary basis. Telephone contacts have their place in setting up a visit, as Chapter 8 will make clear, but beyond that initial contact their value is limited when it comes to establishing a relationship. Of course, once a relationship is established, they are part of the maintenance tools of our time.

Q. What's the biggest mistake congregations make with inactive members?

A. The question ought to be plural, not singular, because there are at least six common mistakes congregations make.

1. Doing nothing—just letting inactive members go.
2. Pushing too hard—taking a results-oriented approach rather than a process-oriented approach.
3. Contacting inactive members to ask for money.
4. Coming in and talking about the needs of the congregation rather than focusing on the needs and concerns of the inactive member.

5. Assuming one knows why the inactive member is inactive—being too quick to generalize. ("All inactive members are lazy; all inactive members just want to have their Sundays free; all....")

6. Using guilt rather than care as the method of ministry.

Q. When is it too late to help?

A. Never. It is never too late to share Christ's love with anyone. Congregations often give up too soon with inactive members. In the first contact with inactive members, there is typically a lot of avoidance on their part. The inactive member is trying to determine whether you really do care. Are you serious? With second and third contacts, the inactive member begins to trust your commitment. Mind you, this opening up can happen in a beginning contact, too, if you genuinely care and come across in a process-oriented way.

Q. What has been proved as the best method to help inactives?

A. The quick answer: Preventing inactivity in the first place is the best way to help inactive members. But once a person has become inactive, the only proved method is personal contact expressed as genuine, selfless, nondemanding care.

Q. Why is personal contact the best method?

A. First, personal contact treats the inactive member as a valuable person. When the inactive member begins to feel valuable to the church, that may be the open door to a first experience of knowing his or her value to God.

Second, when personal contact is genuine and caring, the inactive member does not feel like an object to be collected. The focus is on the real person and that person's needs.

Third, personal contact clears misunderstandings by allowing for the ventilation of feelings.

Fourth and finally, personal contact works because it turns inactive strangers into friends. It builds relationships.

Q. The administrative council replies this way when the question of visiting inactive members comes up: "Pastor, they'll respond better if you go!" What are your views about that?

A. In some instances the pastor certainly might be the more appropriate one to reach out to an inactive member. In others it might better be a lay member of the congregation. In still other instances either one could go.

The point is that *someone* should reach out to inactive members. They should not be treated like hot potatoes tossed back and forth, lest the "potato" grow cold. There is no hard and fast rule as to which is more appropriate. It varies from situation to situation.

Such a response by an administrative council may be a cry for training. It may stem from their perceived inadequacy in meeting the needs of inactive members if they are the ones called on to initiate personal contact. Or they may misunderstand completely the nature of ministry and their relationship to their pastor. They may see their pastor as their "hired hand" whom they pay to take on these supposed burdens of ministry. If this is the case, the administrative council (and likely the whole congregation) needs some thorough education in what the priesthood of all believers is all about.

Q. You say the advisability of having the pastor or a lay person make the contact varies from situation to situation. Could you give some guidelines?

A. One glaring disadvantage of having the pastor be the only one to reach out to inactive members shines forth from a little arithmetic. Take the congregation I mentioned earlier, in which 120 names emerged as potentially inactive, and 41 of those were actually inactive. At 5 minutes apiece to set up a visit and an hour and a half for each visit, including travel time—the total for visiting each person or household only once comes up to 65 hours! Creating a relationship takes much more than one visit, of course, so it ought to be clear that there is far more to do than a pastor alone could manage.

In some cases a visit by the pastor is more appropriate. The authority of the pastoral office carries with it a credibility that the inactive member may need. If the pastor says, "I'm sorry that this happened to you" for a hurt inflicted upon the inactive member, that might have a greater impact.

One advantage to having a lay person reach out, on the other hand, is that the inactive member might be more open and honest with a lay person. People sometimes tell pastors what they think the pastors want to hear. An inactive member also cannot dismiss a lay member's visit as "He (or she) is only doing this because that's his (or her) job." This makes it more likely that the other person's genuine care and concern will come through. One priest told me:

> We have a number of lay members who minister to alienated members of our parish. When I ask them if I should go visit this or that individual to whom we hope to be reconciled, they sometimes say, "It's not time for you yet, Father. When it is, we'll let you know." I rely on their judgment completely.

This priest was patient and sensitive to his role and that of the laity, and ready to let the laity do what they do best!

Notes

1 John S. Savage, "Reactivating the Inactive Member," in *Ministry,* May 1983, p. 27.

2 Kenneth C. Haugk, *Caring for Inactive Members: How to Make God's House a Home,* rev. ed. (1990; St. Louis: Tebunah Ministries, 2004).

5

Seven Steps Your Congregation Can Take

What you know about definition, motivation, and avoiding mistakes prepares you to step out into action. Here are seven steps for you to consider as you think about where you go from here.

Q. What is the first step for a congregation to take in developing an inactive member ministry?

Step 1. Pray

A. There is only one first step, and it is prayer. Pray for inactive members. Pray for yourself, that God will be with you. Pray for the congregation, that it will clearly perceive God's call in this area of ministry.

Piecemeal or erratic ministry often comes about because the motivation of the congregation is not deep enough to carry on a committed, concentrated effort. Prayer will provide a clear mandate and sense of direction from God.

Prayer ought to be interwoven through the whole of your ministry efforts with inactive members, not just at the beginning. Here's what one person I know said:

Prayer is the step I sometimes leave out, and then I wonder why I feel so apprehensive about contacting the inactive person, so fearful about picking up the phone to get in touch with the individual. Without prayer, I forget that God is a part of this process, too, and that God is going to be there helping in so many unseen ways. When I don't pray, I forget that it's God's work instead of mine. Then is when my ego gets tied up in what the outcome is going to be.

You will not lack motivation to pray when you realize the three injuries that church inactivity inflicts: The inactive member suffers, your church suffers, and the world suffers. You are praying for the inactive member's good, the church's good, and the world's good.

Prayer can act as a salve for the anger and judgmentalism many people feel toward inactive members. Part of your prayers—leaders and members alike—must be to turn your anger and judgmentalism over to God in the earnest desire that God will change you.

Which, by the way, God can do.

Martin L. Smith in his book *The Word Is Very Near You* has this to say about prayer:

Prayer is already going on in God. In the love the All-embracing Father has for the Son, and in the love the Son has for the Father, in the issuing of the Spirit from the Father and the Spirit's return in the love of the Son, there is everything we mean by prayer—intimacy, adoration, self-offering, love, desire, crucifyingly acute sympathy for a world torn by pain and joy. Our prayer is not making conversation with God. It is joining the conversation that is already going on in God. . . . There is an eternal dance already in full swing, and we are caught up into it. [1]

Exposure to love of this sort must change us. And it does.

Whom specifically might you pray for? Here are four suitable subjects of your prayers:

1. *Pray for yourself,* that God gives you the strength and ability to listen; that God makes you one who follows through; that God gives you patience and the ability to be present with another, fully with that person in his or her pain.

2. *Pray for the members of your congregation,* that they be hospitable, open, free to welcome all. Pray that they be alert to the early signs of inactivity so that ministry can begin at once.

3. *Pray for your ministry to inactive members,* that you may have courage and wisdom and perseverance and lightheartedness in the task. Pray for the members of any inactive member ministry team you might establish, that they hear God's call and serve with gladness.

4. And finally, *pray for your inactive members,* who are in all probability a huge proportion of your congregation, individuals who in many instances are dealing with crises, concerns, and feelings that cry out for ministry.

Q. After we've prayed, what should we do next?

Step 2. Decide

A. Your congregation, or a significant governing unit within it, needs to make an intentional decision. Otherwise, it's amazing how long an idea can remain in the talking stage and never move beyond that. Gradually it just fades away without any definitive action.

Ask yourself: How well would worship go in your congregation if no one took any initiative to prepare for conducting worship? Intentionality leads to action. Sermons have to be prepared, hymns selected, heat or air-conditioning turned on, and so on. How effective would stewardship drives be in your congregation if no one took the initiative to organize them purposefully? Intentionality leads to action. How well would youth ministry go if no focus or emphasis were placed on it?

It is precisely the same with respect to inactive member ministry: Intentionality leads to action. And intentionality means making a decision that supplying and supporting quality ministry to inactive members is a priority in your congregation.

Quality inactive member ministry has several parts: reaching out to inactive members; learning to welcome inactive members back; and following through on ways to prevent inactivity.

This is the time to make a searching and fearless inventory of your reasons for wanting to begin a ministry to inactive members, or to take a new approach. So often I've seen congregations begin programs of many kinds without first asking themselves the basic questions: Do we really want to do this? Are we willing to pay the price?

I want to stress how important those first two steps are. Prayer is your invitation to God to be part of this process, and your opportunity to hear God's invitation to you. Then, by saying yes to the second-step questions of intentionality (they are deeper questions than you might think), you will have done much to make the rest of the steps easier because your heart is in the right place.

Q. Let's say our congregation has prayed about it, and we have determined we really want to make inactive member ministry a priority. What do we do next?

Step 3. Plan

A. So many times a congregation's next step (or first step) in this area is to recruit a number of (often unwilling) "bounty hunters" who are immediately assigned to contact and cajole inactive members into coming back to church. What a mess this makes!

You need to do some planning first. What are your hopes and expectations? Who is going to be responsible for organizing and following through? Whom are you going to train? How are you going to train?

Carry all your planning out in the spirit recommended by Kennon Callahan, author of *Twelve Keys to an Effective Church.* Callahan said, "The purpose of planning is action. Plan less to achieve more. Plan more and you will achieve less."[2]

In general, depending on the organizational structure of your church, you will need the blessing (preferably enthusiastic participation!) of your pastor and church leadership. The commitment of leadership, if they are not the ones in charge of this effort, will help assure ongoing funding of this program and the continuation of it as a priority effort.

Q. Should all, or at least many, of the members of a congregation be involved in informal ministry to inactive members, or should there be a team of people who work with inactives?

A. This is not an either-or question. The issue of inactivity is so pervasive and complex that any congregation would be well-advised to address the problem on both fronts.

A team of trained individuals could be charged by the congregation with specific outreach and intentional relating to inactive members. Following training and assignments, they ought to meet on an ongoing basis for supervision and support. That specifically focused group is only one part of the puzzle, however. Also crucial is widespread training offered regularly to as many as possible in the congregation. This is the means by which you create a well-informed membership that is alert to early signs of inactivity and ready to step in with thoughtful outreach. You also avoid the unfortunate situation of having an inactive member return, only to leave again when someone's thoughtless or ill-informed remark sabotages much careful ministry.

Probably both general and specific training ought to occur simultaneously. Barring that, offer general training to the congregation first. From those who respond well to this first training, some might form the core of the group that will respond favorably to opportunities for more specific and directed service.

Q. Is it better to set up a special group to reach out to inactive members, or to use an already-constituted group?

A. An already-existing group can certainly do this work, if two conditions are satisfied: 1) The group must not have so much to do already that reaching out to inactive members becomes just one more responsibility; and 2) the group members must really want to be involved in reaching out to inactive members. The first issue relates to how much time the group will spend, the second to whether individuals within the group have the particular interests in this very sensitive ministry.

The answer to this question also depends on the structure and constitution of your congregation. You have to work within that framework. Note this well, however: Whichever kind of group you use, the individuals will have to be trained. Not to do so is to court disaster.

Q. Our congregation enrolled in the Stephen Series system a number of years ago, and we have a successful Stephen Ministry going on now.[3] Could we make caring for inactive members a specialized ministry for some of our Stephen Ministers?

A. Stephen Ministers are recruited and trained with the idea that they minister to individuals who have crises in their lives or are in need of general support. Thus, Stephen Ministers can indeed minister to inactive members who happen to have crises in their lives. In other words, the precipitating reason for the care is not inactivity but the life crises that confront those who happen to be inactive. Under these circumstances, Stephen Ministers would minister to inactive members just as they would anyone else, because there is a felt need.

For Stephen Ministers to be the instrument by which the congregation reaches out intentionally to inactive members *because they are inactive* is another story. You would need to be sure that any Stephen Ministers involved have consented to do this. In addition, Stephen Ministers would require further specialized training before they should attempt such ministry.

Congregations that have both Stephen Ministry and a vital inactive member ministry team are in an ideal position. Those on the inactive member team will be turning up many a member in crisis. These persons will be very willing in most instances to be referred to a Stephen Minister.

Q. Should we focus our efforts on those who have recently become inactive or on those who have been inactive for quite a while?

A. This is a very difficult question because of its moral and ethical overtones. Churches are not immune to the realities of life, which include having to choose how to allocate finite resources. For churches, that may mean a scarcity of willing servants, and for individual Christians that may mean a scarcity of time.

The medical concept of *triage* may be helpful here. Battlefront casualties in time of war or victims of other large-scale catastrophes are hastily assessed and divided into three groups:

- those who in all likelihood will live whether they receive immediate treatment or not;
- those who will have a good chance for recovery if they receive immediate care; and
- those who are likely to die even if they receive immediate care.

On the principle of maximizing the number of survivors, medical personnel will treat the middle group first.

On the same principle of maximizing your efforts, my advice is to concentrate on those who seem most responsive to an initial contact, regardless of the length of time they have been gone. In general this will mean you are focusing your attention on those who have most recently become inactive because they are the ones who still feel the strongest emotional attachment to the church. But there have been some mighty reconciliations with inactive members gone a long time, and these returning members have brought with them some mighty gifts.

The role of Providence in deciding whom you should contact is not to be overlooked either. Prayer, happenstance encounters, and accessibility to specific individuals all play a part in helping you decide whom to minister to first.

Q. Once we have a ministry and awareness plan in place, how do we get people interested and involved?

Step 4. Publicize

A. People will respond, this I assure you, because they have a need to be in ministry, and you will be introducing a way for that need to be satisfied by involving them in relating to inactive members.

Publicity is the bridge between people's need and your offering. It is the way by which congregations can tell the story of what they are about, so that those to whom God is sounding a call can respond to that call.

Your publicity efforts must be phrased in such a way that people see the connection between their need and your program offering. The training experience you offer must be of high quality, and that quality must be evident in how you talk about it.

Q. If we use our channels of communication, won't inactive members be reading and hearing about the program too? How do we guard against raising their anxiety or defensiveness?

A. What you hope is that inactive members will be reading what you say about the training, that they will be hearing about the program. Your publicity can be the beginning of a great witness and outreach to inactive members. Both what you say and the way you say it is the key.

You do not want to communicate a message whose essence is: "We're going out to track down those inactive members and bring 'em back, alive if possible, but any way we can." That kind of results-oriented, uncaring appeal would have disastrous consequences.

You have a golden opportunity to communicate indirectly to inactive members your care about them and your concern about inactivity. The message you want to communicate is this: "We need to address inactivity from every angle possible. We must make our congregation such a loving and caring place that it feels like home to all. We must become a welcoming congregation. We must learn how we can do a better job of relating to inactive members. We must learn to listen, to be sensitive to needs, and to understand others better."

A message like this, which is process-oriented rather than results-oriented, will cause inactive members to feel very positive about what their congregation is doing, and it prepares them for what is to come.

$Q.$ We have so many inactive members, how do we begin?

Step 5. Train

$A.$ Tackling this problem has to be on two levels, both of them related to training. A congregation that really wants to do something about inactive members needs to:

1. Educate as many people as possible in the congregation about inactivity. This will produce good ministry here and there as members have providential encounters with inactive members. It will also do much for prevention as active members learn to be alert for the early signs of inactivity. Finally, it will minimize the likelihood of blunders when inactive members decide to return.

2. Recruit and train an inactive member team who will be charged with the responsibility for intentionally reaching out to specific inactive members.

There are certain key people in a congregation that you ought to make special efforts to reach as part of your periodic offerings of general training. These include Sunday School teachers, elders, deacons, ushers, church staff, the church council, committee leaders and members, small group leaders, and youth leaders. Don't stop with them, however. A vital aspect of this outreach is educating as many of the people of God as possible to be concerned about inactive members. The more people you have relating in healthy ways to inactive members, the better.

Q. Do you have ideas about what this training ought to include to be comprehensive?

A. In the process of putting together the course called *CARING FOR INACTIVE MEMBERS: How to Make God's House a Home,* I gave considerable thought to what such training ought to include. Such a course should be both biblical and practical. It should be feasible for either church staff or selected lay leaders to conduct. The pivotal concept of the course would be its process orientation rather than a results orientation. It should not only be usable for training inactive member teams, but also for educating leaders and congregation members in general.

As an example, here is a partial listing of the contents of that course. [4]

- Attitudes toward inactive members
- Happenstance encounters
- Process-oriented relating
- Causes of inactivity
- Preventing inactivity
- Detecting early inactivity
- Contacting inactive members the first time
- Relating to inactive members
- Inviting inactive members home
- Welcoming them when they do return

As education proceeds in your congregation, perhaps on more than one front, a number of the topics will have far-

---

reaching effects on all other areas of ministry in which the congregation is engaged. For example, *process-oriented relating* is a key concept for every kind of ministry and caring. *Preventing inactivity* will have your leadership groups focusing on ways the congregation can meet everyone's needs better, not just inactive members'. *Detecting early inactivity* presumes an educated and sensitive membership body that is highly tuned in to the first signs of trouble in a person's life. And *relating to inactive members* takes in all sorts of skills that transfer to relating in difficult situations to others.

Q. I can see how an inactive member team could be trained with those concepts. How might others in the congregation be trained?

A. The exact same concepts and practical means of relating are suitable for both general education and specific education of an inactive member team. Education is one of the responsibilities of the local congregation. Matthew 28:19-20 is a command from our Lord to his Church to "go therefore and teach. . . ." Part and parcel of what a congregation must necessarily teach, I believe, is awareness and skills in the area of inactivity—how to relate to inactive members, how to prevent inactivity, and how to welcome home inactive members.

I have a real bias toward education within the congregation that is practical, usable, tangible. People should receive training that is more than just a few facts here and there, which they may or may not use in their lives and ministries in the congregation and beyond. It should be actual, hands-on, skill-based training. Further, when participants learn how to relate effectively to inactive members, they are also learning how to be more caring in all their relationships.

All in all, what I'm talking about is simply good Christian education. You could offer training in any of the settings you ordinarily use. Perhaps that means a special offering in a series of evenings. It may be part of a lay academy you establish—if you haven't already tried one of these, you will be surprised at how people come out for them. Another possibility is training within the regular adult Sunday education session.

Q. How do those who have gone through general education dovetail with the work of an inactive member team?

A. Watch them in action! At Christmas or Easter services, when a high number of inactive members show up, you will see the trained members of your congregation circulating in busy and warm outreach. In effect, they become auxiliary members of the inactive member team.

Some of the people from the general education offerings are also likely to be part of your first inactive member team. You don't have to make this a hard sell. Many are likely to hear this as a call and volunteer for more intentional service. By offering the training periodically—every year, or even more frequently—you will be continually developing new personnel for the team.

Q. Suppose we have established an inactive member team as you suggest, and trained them. To be effective, how many inactive persons should each member of a team relate to?

Step 6. Involve

A. One or two at a time, at most. Perhaps, if the person is retired or otherwise has more time, he or she could be effective with more than this, but otherwise no.

Q. That's a very small number. Wouldn't a congregation be better off reaching out to more people?

A. Relationships take time. What I am advocating is quality care relating. To be sure, if you took a less relational approach, an individual might be able to "handle" five, ten, or even more individuals at a time. But "handling" people is just another way of *manipulating* them.

The question is, do you want to be effective or not? Ten times zero effectiveness is zero, any way you look at it. One or two times one means an effectiveness of one or two. And I am not just talking about *effective* in the sense of "coming back to church," but in the sense of relating in a Christian, loving way.

Look at the impact an inactive member team of, let's say, ten individuals might have over the course of a year. Perhaps each of those ten members of the team relates to one inactive household during a period of three months, four a year. That means that forty of your inactive members will have been warmed by quality outreach during the year. I think that's pretty good, and I have purposely figured conservatively.

There's another factor to be considered here, and it relates to what I call God's economy, by which I mean the multiplication of benefits beyond all measure when God's hand is at work. Here's what one individual said, by way of illustration:

Sandra was a very marginal member in our church, attending maybe half a dozen times a year. A few years back another woman and I started a single women's support group, figuring to deal with those in the age-range of 20-45. But Sandra, who was 60, asked if it would be okay for her to attend. As she became fully involved in that group, she began to attend church more and more regularly. Soon she also started bringing other people to our group. One of her friends, an inactive member from another church that had disbanded several years ago, joined our church. Then this person's inactive son and his family joined our church. The cycle of outreach still continues: Sandra is still bringing people into our church.

The whole point of this is that by ministering fully and completely to one inactive member, you will find benefits multiplying many times over as that person reaches out to minister too, and the person that person reaches then reaches out. When God is with you, who shall be against you?

$Q.$ What do you do with an individual who wants to be involved in purposive relating to inactive members, but who is ill-suited for it?

$A.$ The purpose of training is to equip those for ministry who are otherwise not that well-equipped. No amount of training, however, will equip someone who is ill-suited to the task. For example, you do not want to have someone who is negative, aggressive, or extremely pushy as your congregation's point of contact with inactive members.

Gently and firmly encourage these individuals to become involved in other activities of the church that might more closely suit their gifts. There is no harm in offering training to these people—in fact, such an educational experience will possibly help them to discover for themselves what type of ministry is for them. Better yet, it may turn out that their "unsuitability" was just a matter of being untrained. If they are still unsuitable, however, and they don't make that decision themselves, then your firmness is essential. The spiritual welfare of a number of individuals may be at stake.

$Q.$ In formalizing the involvement of individuals to contact inactive members, is it better to have men relate to men and women to women?

$A.$ Yes. When an individual has become inactive, he or she is in a type of crisis. In this state, mixing gender can add a variable that may hinder the building of a relationship. An inactive member has a lot of thoughts and feelings about his or her inactivity, which makes the situation sensitive enough without having to deal with the cross-gender issues of relationship.

Q. What kind of prior relationship is best between inactive members and the ones who might visit them? Should they be well-acquainted, minor acquaintances, or total strangers?

A. It's less important where the relationship begins, more important where it goes. The common mistake is to believe that a close prior relationship is necessary. It isn't. Even "strangers" to one another share the commonalities of belonging to the same congregation and being Christians, and these factors make a six-lane bridge to walk over and meet someone.

Q. How do individuals involved in visiting inactive members keep their spirits up?

Step 7. Support

A. Any individuals who are involved in purposive and consistent reaching out to inactive members as part of their responsibilities need to meet together on a continuing basis for support, consultation, and affirmation.

These meetings are not simply "business" meetings. In the time they spend together, team members should very specifically focus on themselves—their feelings, what they have done right, what they might have done wrong, and so on. There should be a definite leader, probably (but not necessarily) the pastor. The leader's role is one of serious guidance, keeping people in focus and on track. The leader makes sure everyone who has need gets a chance to talk. The leader makes sure that the atmosphere remains one of encouragement, affirmation, and support.

Another lift to group spirits will be the fact that the group is operating from a process orientation rather than a results orientation. With the pressure of "having to get results" taken away, the morale of the group will be buoyant.

Q. How often should these support sessions meet?

A. Once a month is probably enough, with twice monthly an option. You will have to adapt this to your own circumstances and your team members' desires. Don't be afraid of having high expectations. People want training; they want tangible support. They will go out of their way to get it.

Q. What exactly should go on during these meetings?

A. A number of different experiences can go on.

1. *Supervision and support.* At least three team members each session should have a chance to present their caring relationship and get help from their peers and the leader or leaders as to how they're doing and how they should proceed. This should probably take no more than ten or fifteen minutes each.

2. *Continuing education.* Further training for the team members in relationship skills such as reflective listening and drawing out feelings; help with the skills of being assertive from a Christian standpoint, as has already been mentioned; and Bible study to keep the team focused on Who is in charge and Who is the one to whom the credit should go when inactive members decide to return.

3. *Personal sharing.* Team members should have a chance to share their thoughts and feelings—both highs and lows. Some will bring frustration, many will bring celebration as they experience the joy of being Christ to the ones they call on.

4. *Administration.* There will also be a certain amount of administrative work—the leader should be checking in to see how often the team members are calling on their inactive members, and whether anyone needs a new assignment.

5. *Prayer support.* Team members and leaders need to know what God can teach through prayer—that they

are loved, that God is with them, that Christ is already in the inactive member ready to unite with the Christ in them. All inactive member ministry takes place under the guidance of the Holy Spirit, to bring about the will of the Lord. What is God's will? Let Jesus respond to that: "So it is not the will of your Father in heaven that one of these little ones should be lost" (Matthew 18:14).

All these will keep morale high and contribute substantively to the improved ability of the team members to relate to inactive members. These gatherings should take place in an atmosphere of affirmation, with everyone accountable for attendance and with a commitment from all to pray for each other and the inactive members they are ministering to. A time for food and friendship is always a good idea, perhaps in a break between supervision and continuing education. Much mutual ministry and informal learning can take place amidst coffee and cookies.

Q. What about confidentiality—how do I know what's pertinent and what isn't appropriate to share in the team meetings?

A. Here are some guidelines for you.

- *Don't* mention to team members the inactive member's name, or the names of family members.
- *Don't* tell team members something the inactive member asked you not to tell.
- *Don't* share with the other team members intimate details of the inactive member's life that have no bearing at all on the ministry relationship.
- *Don't* tell people outside of the team about the ministry relationship.
- *Don't* mention the inactive member's name or details about the ministry relationship during public prayers or testimony.
- *Don't* reveal the inactive member's identity in order

to obtain other kinds of help for him or her, unless you have his or her permission.

Q. In developing a quality relationship with an inactive member, is it possible to become personally overextended with one individual?

A. It certainly is, and this is another instance where good, ongoing quality ministry assurance can help. The group may be able to gently point the team member's attention to the question: Whose needs are being fulfilled? Is it the inactive member's needs for ministry that are being met, or the active member's need to be a rescuer, a savior?

More often than not, the active member will experience the inactive member as somewhat distant and aloof rather than as too clinging. The case might be different should the person decide to return to church. Then is when expectations might differ. The active member may see this as the time for beginning disengagement, while the formerly inactive person expects the same kind of involvement as before. This is another good reason why the whole congregation needs to be involved and readied for the process of re-assimilating inactive members.

To summarize the steps you follow, they are: (1) Pray (2) Decide (3) Plan (4) Publicize (5) Train (6) Involve (7) Support. These seven steps form the core of an organizational scheme that will ensure that the ministry you establish is consistent, committed, and effective.

Notes

1 Martin L. Smith, *The Word Is Very Near You: A Guide to Praying with Scripture* (Cambridge, MA: Cowley, 1989).

2 Kennon L. Callahan, *The Leader's Guide: Twelve Keys to an Effective Church* (San Francisco: Harper & Row, 1987).

3 For information about the Stephen Series system of lay caring ministry, write Stephen Ministries, 2045 Innerbelt Business Center Drive, St. Louis, MO 63114-5765 or call (314) 428-2600.

4 Kenneth C. Haugk, *Caring for Inactive Members: How to Make God's House a Home,* rev. ed. (1990; St. Louis: Tebunah Ministries, 2004).

6

Sensitivity and Understanding

"Let there be such oneness between you that when
one cries, the other tastes salt."

Salt is a rich source of metaphor in language. "You are the
salt of the earth" (Matt. 5:13), Jesus says to the faithful, whom
he has just described in the Beatitudes. You are what can give
the food of life its savor, he means. Applying this to inactive
members, it is a happy image: You are what will make inactive
members' participation in the community of believers a well-
seasoned banquet.

Sensitivity and understanding are two essentials of a quality
relationship, a salty relationship in the sense that Jesus meant.
Too often, however, these characteristics are minimally present
or altogether absent in the relationship between active members
and inactive members. Instead, active members have proceeded
as if they were "salt to be rubbed into another's wounds,"
another metaphor but one with not so happy connotations.
The inactive member is in pain; he or she is almost certainly
wounded in some way. To rub salt in that wound, to approach
the individual without sensitivity and understanding, is to
multiply that person's pain. Such activity by faithful Christians

has never been acceptable, and now, equipped as you are with a process orientation to relating, you have an alternative.

Q. Is it ever appropriate to go talk to someone specifically because he or she is inactive?

A. Yes, it is appropriate. Appropriate? It is necessary! It is imperative!

Your question is posed very well. There is a major difference between the question you asked and the one you could have asked. Your question treats inactivity quite properly as a symptom. The question suggests that you are a person who wants to find out what is going on. This is a process-oriented question.

You could have asked instead, Is it appropriate to go talk to an individual *about* his or her inactivity? That question seems to assume that inactivity in and of itself is the problem. It suggests that the one who asks it is already certain of what is going on and is ready to deliver some solutions. It is a results-oriented question, and to it the answer is "No, it is highly inappropriate."

But to go talk to someone *because* of the person's inactivity? Absolutely.

Q. What is it that inactive members most need to hear?

A. They don't need to hear anything. They need to be heard.

Q. I'm embarrassed to get in touch with some of our inactive members. The congregation hasn't been in touch with them for months or even years. What's the best way to show concern for people who have been left out in the cold like this?

A. You are correct, there are inactive members who have been left out in the cold, and the best way to remedy that is with relaxed warmth. Just visit them. Ask, "How are things going with you?" Ask, "How have you been doing?"

Notorious neglect by your congregation might warrant your showing up at the inactive member's door wearing sackcloth and ashes. What do I mean by *notorious neglect?* I mean instances where the "preponderance of evidence" clearly suggests that inertia or inaction on the part of the congregation has resulted in people not being reached out to who should have been.

I suppose I'm kidding about the sackcloth and ashes, but just barely. For sure, you can apologize. In cases of notorious neglect, the words *I'm sorry* can be the most powerful words you could say to the inactive member.

You may think, "But I have no right to apologize for the congregation." Sure you do. You are a member of the Body of Christ. That body is a unity, not a bunch of little disconnected cells, each living isolated and independent lives. An injury to one is an injury to all.

Above all, be honest. If the person has been neglected, and you know it, you can be sure the neglected one knows it too. Therein lies the explanation for the inactive person's anger that sometimes comes out during the first or second visit. Don't take this anger personally. It may be directed at you, but it's not meant for you. It is anger that has to come out before reconciliation and healing can take place.

Many times congregations and their leaders know that they should have been contacting inactive members, and they feel justly guilty for their failings. Satan triumphs when these guilty feelings create a conspiracy of silence that prevents any outreach at all.

Don't worry too much in advance about the best way to make an approach—just make it. Relate to inactive members as fellow human beings, seriously, but not with white-knuckle intensity.

Q. Is there usually one main reason why people become inactive, or multiple reasons?

A. There is typically a cluster of reasons that leads one to become inactive. These reasons can include personal crises, problems with interpersonal relations, and not getting one's needs met. Most of the time these causes accumulate over time. Often, however, the latest one becomes "the straw that broke the camel's back," and that becomes the one to which the inactive member points. Here's the way one individual explains it:

> Inactivity is very complex, and in many cases we inactive members will point to a certain recent event as the cause because that is what we honestly believe is the cause. It is only when talk peels away the layers that we become aware of how much more was involved. It is not that we were hiding the true reasons from the active member, but that we were so close to the problem we were unable to get a clear view.

Causes may be either personal or institutional—that is, they may be events, circumstances, and attitudes connected with inactive individuals' lives, or they may relate to factors within the congregation itself. Because causes do come in clusters, often both personal and institutional factors are at the root of a person's inactivity.

Q. Where does spiritual health come in? That is, what's the relationship between being inactive and being a good Christian?

A. The great majority of people who become inactive do so for reasons and combinations of reasons that are not explicitly spiritual in nature. As I have mentioned, they become inactive for relational, social, psychological, and family reasons, or personal and family crises. It is a gross misconception to assume that most inactivity is caused by a waning of faith. That just isn't so. Here's what one formerly inactive member said:

> My faith meant very much to me both before and during the time I was inactive. My faith mattered so

much precisely because I felt spiritually betrayed and disillusioned. Was I an inferior Christian, or a spiritually apathetic or disinterested person? No way! I cared, but I felt both God and my fellow church members had let me down when I was hurting from too many situations I couldn't understand. I didn't know how to draw on any resources to gain strength for coping with all these problems that had suddenly descended upon me.

The major question is a ministry one, not an analytic or judgmental one: What can be done? How can I help see that this person's needs are met? We really need to watch carefully our possible arrogance in this particular area. Our attitudes can set us up for doing some abominable "ministry"—haranguing the inactive member about faith—that isn't ministry at all.

Q. How active is the devil in the business of causing inactivity?

A. The devil is very active indeed, I would say—100% of the time. The next question is, where is the devil working? In whom? In a fallen world, alas, the answer is, "In all of us." The devil may be fomenting strife in the congregation, creating situations ripe for inconsiderateness toward others. Personal crises in a member's life may be due to the work of the devil. The inactive member may also be having a crisis of faith.

The good news, in this universe that belongs to God (no matter how the devil might wish it otherwise), is that God's Holy Spirit is also in us. This means that what has been loosed by deviltry can be leashed and tamed by loving members of Christ's own Body—the Church. This means the devil's lie—"you can always do it tomorrow"—can be thrown back in his face by loving actions today.

Q. But you can't deny that sin is operating in the inactive member, can you?

A. I can't deny that sin is operating in anyone. The theology I have internalized—with joy and thanksgiving, I might add—is that Jesus' death was necessary for me to be reconciled with God because I am a sinner. In workshops when this question comes up, I throw out an invitation to all: "Raise your hand if you're perfect." No one ever has yet.

Inactive members and the church need to be reconciled, and that's a mutual task. Reconciliation is a two-way street. The inactive member and the church come toward each other—Jesus has prepared a banquet table where all can sit and feast. When you perceive that reconciliation is needed, you will be led to look also within yourself for the needs of healing and forgiveness you have. In Isaiah 43:19, God says to the church as much as the inactive member, "I am about to do a new thing; now it springs forth, do you not perceive it?"

Q. Christ invites us to worship, so isn't a rejection of worship a rejection of Christ?

A. Although a failure to attend worship may mean a rejection of Christ, it does not follow as an absolutely necessary consequence. Frequently there are precipitating circumstances, sometimes excruciating in their violence, that create a situation for a person that makes inactivity seem like the best available option. One person who attended a workshop I gave on church inactivity said:

> This workshop challenged me to focus on people and their needs rather than their failure to "Remember the Sabbath Day, and keep it holy."

I couldn't have said it better myself! By the way, attendance at worship does not guarantee Christian behavior either. Active

members who have been the offending ones, have caused a fellow
member some hurt, may equally well be the ones who have
rejected Christ. Jesus himself had something to say about this:

> "Occasions for stumbling are bound to come, but woe
> to anyone by whom they come! It would be better for
> you if a millstone were hung around your neck and
> you were thrown into the sea than for you to cause
> one of these little ones to stumble."
>
> Luke 17:1b-2

This business of pointing the finger at someone's faith,
especially in advance before any listening has gone on, is very
risky. I may find out that the finger is pointing at me. Jesus
again:

> "Why do you see the speck in your neighbor's eye,
> but do not notice the log in your own eye?"
>
> Luke 6:41

Q. You keep stressing that inactive members need a great
deal of care, a listening ear, and other ministry. When do
inactive members begin to be more concerned about giving than
getting?

Q. I admit there is the need for compassion, sensitivity,
understanding, and all that, but when do inactive members face
up to the necessity of their own commitment and discipleship?

A. These questions betray the old attitudes of judgmentalism with which active church members have typically viewed
inactive members. When an animal is seriously injured, often
it will "den up" in some secret spot, there to await either death
or recovery. This is self-centered behavior, for the sake of
survival, but that does not make it selfish behavior. Inactive
members have often suffered serious hurts of one kind or
another, and their inactivity may be their "denning up" for
survival. Often active members interpret this as selfishness, but
it need not be.

What gets people through such times is ministry, nurture, care. Only after they have received what they need to survive will it be possible for them to "take up the cross" again. And then they often do so with amazing power. They often become what Henri Nouwen calls "wounded healers," ones who by the depths of their own suffering have been equipped to be powerful healers of others.[1]

Q. What are some ways active members contribute to others' inactivity?

A. "How do I hurt thee? Let me count the ways": By criticizing. By giving people dirty looks when their child makes noise in church. By ignoring. By being intolerant of differences. By not recognizing someone. Whatever comes to mind for you, about how one person can hurt another, that's the answer, because for some those hurts can lead to inactivity.

Q. Heavens, if everyone would quit the church because of hurt feelings, there would be no one left! Shouldn't those who have become inactive because of hurt feelings have a thicker skin? Thank goodness everyone is not so thin-skinned.

A. The ones who let criticism roll off them like water off a duck's back—these people are indeed unique. But my own strongest *thank goodnesses* are reserved for something else. Thank goodness God did not say, "Shouldn't I wait to bestow salvation until humans merit it?" We'd all be doomed. No one of us deserves salvation.

The same is true for our charge to be holy lovers. We do not love others because they deserve to be loved—they do not, any more than we do. We love *because we have been loved,* by God. It would be nice if fallenness did not exist in the world, but it does. That is the way the world is. That is, in fact, the way humans are, as St. Paul says:

> For I know that nothing good dwells within me, that

is, in my flesh. I can will what is right, but I cannot do it.

Romans 7:18

No amount of telling injured, suffering people the way they should be does anything to change them. Change occurs by God's actions when people have been loved enough to have strength enough to be weak—that is, to let down their defenses against God.

Here's the way one formerly inactive member puts it.

> If I had only a few words to say to active members, this is what I'd say: "Don't condemn us. Just care. Help us to believe again that God loves us as much as he loves you."

Q. How can you tell what people's needs are?

A. Just ask them. If you ask, really mean it when you ask, and then keep your mouth closed and your ears open, most inactive members will tell you their needs, their hurts, their complaints—most anything you need to know to be well-informed in your relating to them.

Churches ought to be asking people about their needs long before they become inactive. It never ceases to amaze me that congregations often go through an elaborate new-member-orientation process, and that nowhere in this process is there any evidence that the congregation is interested in the new member's needs. Instead, it's usually a one-way flow of information: "Here is a list of the slots we need people to fill. What shall we sign you up for?"

I've heard it said, "But if we ask inactive members what their needs are, they won't tell us." Not true. They will tell you if you have asked and are obviously receptive. Sometimes the way you ask can make a lot of difference. If you give the impression you are waiting to pounce on whatever the inactive person says, ready to tear the person's words to shreds, then you are right, you are unlikely to get an answer.

If you are feeling judgmental inside, then judgmental tones of voice and judgmental body postures will give you away even when your words are correct. The converse is true, too. If you are genuinely concerned for the other, you will communicate caring even when you err in the words you choose.

Q. How do you balance an individual's needs with the purpose of the Gospel?

A. Evidently you think an individual's true needs and the Gospel might be at cross purposes. I don't. I think they coincide. How could it be otherwise? The purpose of the Gospel is to announce the good news of God's saving grace, reconciliation, justification, and sanctification of humankind. This is good news precisely because it is what every individual—active or not—truly needs.

Q. I agree that it is important to fulfill needs. But some individuals have totally unrealistic needs. If the congregation panders to every need people express, won't it be trying to be all things to all people?

A. Most inactive members have needs that are very down-to-earth, needs for basic ministry and being equipped for ministry. It is really the exception when someone's needs are unrealistic.

The concern implicit in this question is for mostly hypothetical kinds of instances: What if the person expects a chauffeured limousine to pick him or her up for church? A 17-piece orchestra at every worship service?

"Mostly hypothetical," I said. Sometimes a person can have an unrealistic expectation of the church—for instance, that the pastor would visit him or her every day, or every week. Although you and I quickly recognize that this is unreasonable, it may represent a very real need of the person for nurture and relationship. If that is the need, there may be other ways the need could be satisfied. One silent question for an active member always to be asking, with a prayerful request for discernment: "Lord, what is the real need this person has, and how can we hope to respond to it?"

Q. Are inactive members less likely to return if they have been away for a longer period of time?

A. Yes, they are. There is a direct relationship—the longer people have been away from church, the less likely they are to return. During the first couple of months, inactive members are very open to coming back, and even more open to having someone from church contact them. After that they distance or detach themselves more. Relating to them will be more difficult, although not impossible. This is why it is so important to have early detection systems set up so you know who is inactive and can get in touch with them.

Q. What are some of the early signals that indicate an individual might be becoming inactive?

A. There are many different ways to tell ahead of time, or in the very early stages:

- Spotty attendance
- Changes in giving habits
- Changes in program participation
- Talk about leaving
- Diminished dependability

Sometimes people will say in so many words that they are thinking of dropping out of church involvement. Another early signal is that the person gives just a hint of some kind of crisis in his or her personal life. This may be a testing, or a cry for help. The person may be waiting to see if anyone is going to follow up on this hint and ask for more information. If no support is forthcoming, that may be the impetus the person needs to conclude that this congregation does not care and is not the place for him or her. Inactivity may be the consequence.

Q. When people are inactive because of a relational issue, but spiritually they're doing all right, why don't they join another congregation?

A. Spiritually they're probably not doing all right—spiritually they're probably hurting. Something has gone awry in the place they have counted on for security and love. What now? Walk into another setting where the same thing might happen?

More importantly, they are certain to still feel ties to the congregation they have absented themselves from, and those ties are not casually or easily severed. Their bond—however strained—is the great source of hope and impetus for action for the congregation as it looks at its ministry to inactive members. In every important sense, it is not only the congregation that hopes for the return of inactive members, but also the inactive members themselves wanting to return.

Note

1 Henri J. M. Nouwen, *The Wounded Healer* (Garden City, NY: Image Books, 1979).

7

Special Concerns

Grouped in this chapter are questions about special situations that made it difficult for the questioners to see how to proceed. Clearing up these questions now will enable you to deal with the practical aspects of later chapters without the distraction of "Yes, but what if...?"

Q. How do we reactivate burned-out members?

A. Basically, you don't and you can't. All you can do is help create an environment in which burned-out members may reactivate themselves. Listen to them, care for them, love them. The very act of doing this will minister to these individuals at their point of greatest need. Assure them almost with the rigor of a formal covenant that you will not allow overextension to happen to them again. To the extent that you have control over the situation, protect them from future overuse and abuse.

Recognize the work they did, saying, "What you did was fantastic." Encourage them to say no to protect themselves, and offer yourself as coach and cheerleader to help. If they are burned out in the congregation to the point of becoming inactive, there is a good chance this characteristic is evident in the rest of their life as well. There may be courses in assertiveness training available that you can steer them to, or you can suggest they read a book that teaches them assertiveness from a Christian perspective, such as *Speaking the Truth in Love: How to Be an Assertive Christian.* [1] By teaching them and equipping them in the arena of the church, you will be helping them in all the other arenas, too—family, work, and community.

Q. What do you do or say when a new member immediately becomes inactive? In such instances, when we've asked, the individuals have said they were just premature in joining. How do we bring them back?

Q. There are two types of inactive members as I see it: the previously active who drops out and the never-been-active. How do we reach out to those latter individuals?

A. You need to take a good, close look at your congregation and what it does or doesn't do to assimilate new members. The individuals you describe have evidently never bonded with the congregation. This is good news because it represents a marvelous opportunity to do something about it. Assimilation is in your control to a great extent. Bonding takes place, as Lyle Schaller points out, because individuals already have a cluster of friends or relatives in the congregation, or because they get involved in a relationship-building group right away. Bonding can also take place when a new member takes on a role (elected to an office, for example) or a task that provides a sense of belonging and identity. [2]

Bonding needs to take place quite soon after a member joins. Your congregation must establish mechanisms to be sure that everyone who joins has maximum opportunity for bonding quickly.

Q. Is there any hope at all for people who have been inactive for a long time?

A. What I hope comes through loud and clear is that there really is hope for everyone—if only we will begin! To be sure, when an individual has been gone "a long time"—whether that means one year, or two, or ten—the expectation that he or she will return is considerably lessened. But never give up hope. Here is confirmation from another formerly inactive member:

> Thank heaven Jesus didn't come to Earth, size up us incorrigible human beings, and say, "It's hopeless. There's no sense in going to the cross for these creatures. It won't make any difference." I pray we learn to be like our faithful Savior and not prejudge who is reachable and who is not. We must stop writing people off as hopeless.

It just might be that the congregation has never really reached out to the person in a personal way. Such a personal gesture can be the catalyst for an inactive member's return. Even if the person does not come back, your ministry will have been a very positive living out of the Gospel.

Q. How do you get people more involved who attend worship and contribute financially, but are otherwise not active?

A. Talk with them about their lives—highs and lows, issues of concern, their view of the church, and their relationship with God. The purpose of such an interaction is exploratory, listening and learning. The purpose should have nothing to do with harassment or judgment. Relate to these individuals in a non-threatening way, and avoid coming down on them regarding their level of involvement. Be positive and affirming of them as persons.

Through conversations such as these, you will find out a lot about these individuals—what their needs are and how they can be challenged. Many times people are not involved more fully within congregations because the opportunities for involvement are not what interest them. You might think, "Well, they should shape up and get interested," but you are writing a script for defeat if you take that attitude. I have noted many times in my work that congregations that begin recruiting for effective lay caring, as an example, often find that many of those who respond are people who have not been very active in the church for ten or fifteen years. When the church offers opportunities for involvement that are really meaningful for them, then these people do get involved.

Q. What do you do about members who support the congregation financially, but do not attend?

A. Curiously enough, financial support is sometimes the last to go when someone is beginning to detach and become inactive. First is participation in special programs and activities; second is worship; and only afterward does the person discontinue contributing. This certainly suggests that the person still feels a commitment or bond to the congregation, which suggests that going to talk with the person may be a very caring act.

Q. How do you deal with "two-timing Christians," i.e., those who only come to church on Christmas and Easter and still wish to be considered members?

A. You can start by rejoicing in the fact that they are not "no-timers." As long as they are attending even this minimal amount, they are approaching the Gospel and placing themselves in a position to be acted upon by God's Word and the warmth of your witness.

Train as many active members as possible to avoid making matters worse with these individuals. No caustic, snide remarks, please. I heard of one instance when an infrequent worshipper came to a Christmas Eve service and the usher promptly made a big show of holding up the church wall because he "was afraid the roof was going to fall in." Such sarcasm will almost certainly ensure that the individual will not be back before next Christmas Eve, if then.

Welcome the person warmly (not gushily) and relate to him or her in a friendly, caring, hospitable fashion. Tell the individuals you're glad to see them. Whatever you do, don't shun them. These special festivals of the Christian church are a golden opportunity to let the light of Christ's love shine equally on active and inactive members.

In addition to relating in a high quality way at church, you can also follow up with these individuals. Give them a call and suggest getting together just to find out how things are going for them. The subject of church may or may not arise in such a contact. In any case, it will not be your purpose to talk about church, though you will certainly be willing to if the other wants to.

I like the way one pastor treated this situation in a church newsletter right after Easter:

> It felt good to see so many friends in church last Sunday. Some of you were back visiting from out of town and others revisited their "home" church after being gone for a while. I'm glad so many came to worship on Easter Sunday. I look forward to your return. Many worked very hard so your visit would be enjoyable.

One priest at a Roman Catholic conference on church inactivity I attended put it this way:

> We don't throw rocks at "C and E" Christians anymore.

Q. There are several active members in our congregation whose spouses never attend. They say that no one understands their situation. What can we do in these cases?

Q. Do the active family members of an inactive person have any unique ministry needs? What can other members of the congregation do to help them and be supportive of their continued involvement?

A. They deserve every admiration for their persistence in participation. It's not easy on a beautiful Sunday morning to leave one's home for church when your inactive spouse, for example, is sipping coffee on the terrace and reading the newspaper in comfortable clothes. It's not easy to go off to church if you are a child and neither of your parents supports your interest.

Don't badger the active member about where the missing family member is. The person is feeling lonely enough without that. Do let the individual know how glad you are to see him or her. Offer companionship in the pew, an offer that will be especially welcome for a parent if there are small children involved.

The individual who says others don't understand may be exactly right. Put yourself in the active person's shoes for a moment, as reported by one individual:

> When I do come to church, it seems like I'm sitting alone but everyone else comes into the church two by two. If I bring the children, there's no one but me to keep them orderly and quiet. If you have more than two kids, you run out of sides to put them on to keep them separated and out of mischief! All these pressures may be compounded by someone's dirty looks at the children.
>
> My nonattending spouse sometimes sabotages my desire to go to church, too. This can take the form of overtly aggressive behavior such as yelling and fighting, ridiculing religion, complaining about the amount of money given to church, or outright refusal to allow me to attend. Passive resistance is another form of sabotage in which my spouse refuses to watch the children, schedules other activities at the time of worship services, or neglects shared family responsibilities.

Wearing those shoes is uncomfortable, isn't it? You begin to see how hard it could be for a spouse of a nonattending individual to attend, how easy to cease participation.

A listening and caring ministry is never out of place. The active member is very likely to wish he or she had someone to talk to about the difficulties in the situation. If you felt compelled to deliver answers, you might be reluctant to assume the role of such ministry, but it's not your mouth that is required. It's your ears.

Q. Is there some particular way to reach out to the inactive spouse in these instances?

A. Here's a couple of ideas that can work:

1. Schedule special events to which the active member can invite his or her inactive spouse. This shouldn't be too hard—churches are always putting on talent shows, musical events, children's services, suppers, and the like. Make it a particular point to suggest to the active one that he or she invite the spouse. (It can also be beneficial if some of these events don't take place at church: a potluck supper at someone's home is an example.) Other active people at these events need to be on their best *trained* behavior. Here's where training as many people as possible in the congregation can really pay dividends. You don't want someone greeting the inactive person with some such inane remark as, "Oh, here's beauty and the beast—guess which one's the beast."

2. One pastor I know makes it a point to contact the inactive spouses and have lunch with them. The purpose is not to do a hard sell, work them over, or browbeat them, but just to get to know them. What has often happened is that the inactive member no longer saw the church as a competitor, and there was relaxation of tensions on the homefront for the active member. In some instances the development of a relationship

opened the door for the inactive members to start coming to church. As that pastor said, "If someone comes back to church, that is great, but I am always very clear in my own mind that I am not setting out with that goal in mind. My goal is simply to get to know the individual and give him or her a chance to get to know me as a person."

Q. Some family members have trouble returning to the church after a funeral. What causes that? What can be done about it?

A. After a death (and after a divorce, too), it can be very painful to be in familiar settings without a familiar person beside you. Either one of these situations can create major and ongoing stresses: emotional, economic, spiritual, physical, and social. These can add up to a continuing crisis state that necessitates high-quality care, preferably from the church or including the church.

The emotional stresses in particular are related to grieving. Many things can touch off tears, for example, and the person may have a horror of "making a spectacle" of him- or herself. There is a desolated sense of aloneness. The person feels disconnected. After spending the energy required for grieving, there isn't much left over for mustering up the strength to return to church.

As the shock and pain wear off, worry sets in: What will become of me? These anxieties are related to the economic effects. The necessity for a job, a second job, even a third job can make it difficult for the person to attend church.

In addition, there are the spiritual effects. Depending upon the stage of grief one is in, a person may be gripped by anger at God for allowing this tragedy to happen and feel unworthy or unwilling to be in church as a result.

All these effects can cause physical problems as well. The individual may become literally "sick with grief," and during the recovery get out of the habit of coming to church. The longer a person is out of touch, especially when there are not regular, caring visits by church members, the harder it may be for that person to return.

You may be tempted to dismiss the social effects as minimal compared with the others, but grieving individuals may feel these effects most sharply when they return to church. They are alone. Where should they sit? How do others relate to them now that they are alone, when before they were always in the company of someone else? Subtly and not so subtly others often give off signals that they no longer have the same relationship.

All the preceding is related to the part of your question about causes. The answer to the second question is much more brief. What can be done about it? Provide good Christian care to these individuals.

When the Inactive Person
Is a Family Member

Q. There is a member of my family who is inactive, and I am very concerned. How do you deal with inactivity in your own family without sounding too preachy or pushy?

Q. An inactive member of our congregation is a member of my family. I feel very inadequate. What do I do?

A. The same principles of caring and listening apply, but when an inactive member is related to you, the dynamics in play create a special situation requiring special treatment. Your greater personal investment adds a difficulty to the process for you. Because your contacts with family members are so much more frequent than they would be with other inactive members, you have to be especially careful to bite your tongue sometimes, not say anything even when you're itching to. It's not easy to be quiet when you care so much.

Start with prayer. This is more a matter of reminding yourself who's in charge than it is badgering God with importunities to do something. About your teen-aged son, as an example, you have to say repeatedly, for your own benefit, "God, I place so-and-so in your hands. I know I cannot change him. I know I cannot make him come to church, no matter how much I might wish it. Give me the good sense to accept and love him as he is, and communicate that acceptance and love to him."

Meanwhile, continue to engage in your church activities as you have been. Be a role model for the person. Be as genuinely and fully functioning a Christian as you can—with dedication that comes from the very center of your being, not a veneer on the outside.

You can issue mild invitations to special events, but not continually, and not sharply. No bullhorns at 7:00 A.M. Sunday mornings: "You lazy so-and-so! Get up and go to church with me or I'll disown [divorce] you!" That is not the best way to invite someone to church. Lean more to casual invitations: "Would you like to go?" If by chance the person does accompany you to some special event, don't say, "I hope you come back again and again and again." Instead, say simply, "Glad you came. It was really nice being with you at church tonight." Period. Close your mouth. Sew it shut. Don't say another word.

Another way to proceed: Have someone in the individual's peer group be the contact. Here is how that worked for one individual.

> This is what I did with my mother. I got in touch with the president of one of our women's circles and asked her if she would take my heart concern to the women in her circle and see if they would befriend my mother. It was actually their actions, which spanned about a year's time, that brought her back into the church. They were able to do what I as a daughter could not have done.

When the Inactive Member
Is a Close Friend

Q. How do you talk with personal friends about their inactivity without coming across as superior?

A. Just as inactive family members place special considerations upon those who would relate to them, so too with close friends. The good news is that the relationship is already there; the bad news is the difficulties this sometimes causes in reaching out to them.

Your attitude to begin with is the key. If you are feeling superior, you won't come across as humble no matter how hard you try. Search your heart. If you're a real friend, you are the servant of your friend, not an equal and not a superior. You are reaching up to Jesus Christ, who resides in him or her.

Q. I have a friend who used to be a member at my church and even attended Sunday School there. This friend has now become active in a non-Christian religion. How can I witness to my friend?

A. Certainly, to jump right in with a presentation of the claims of the Christian faith would be irresponsible. Rather, you should learn something about the new religion. Then, should the time come when your friend indicates a willingness to talk, you will be better prepared to give "an accounting for the hope that is in you" (1 Peter 3:15). If you do get a chance to talk to your friend, find out how it happened that he or she changed religions. Knowing where your friend is spiritually will help you tailor your responses to his or her situation.

Sometimes when people are around non-Christians they tend to put on a few extra Christian layers, showing off. Don't do that—almost always it comes across as phony. More likely than not your friend would see such behavior for what it is, an act, and be confirmed in his or her new faith. Simply be the new creature God has made you.

Witness to your friend through your life and actions. Jesus said, "Let your light shine before others, so that they may see your good works and give glory to your Father in heaven" (Matthew 5:16). God's role for you may be to let your light shine, and that's all. Your friend may not wish to talk with you about his or her new beliefs, and for you to force the issue would probably do more harm than good. But there's nothing wrong with showing interest in your friend's new faith. This may be the opening he or she needs to begin to talk to you about it.

Remember that you are not God's only instrument for bringing your friend to Christ. Paul writes to the church at Corinth, "I planted, Apollos watered, but God gave the growth" (1 Corinthians 3:6). We would do well to realize that God still gives the growth and we are merely instruments in his hands.

Q. How do you approach good friends who chose to leave the church years ago?

A. With friends it's okay to bring up the subject of inactivity yourself, so long as you're not hounding them. This is a basic difference from a visit to an inactive member who is not a good friend. There, you wait for the inactive member to bring up the subject himself or herself. (For more about this, see Chapter 13.) But with friends, there is certainly nothing wrong in talking with them about their church involvement, as long as you are not trying to tell them what to do. Meanwhile, just go on being friends with them, and be the loving embodiment of Jesus Christ to them at the same time. That's who you are.

A Special Case: Church Antagonists

Q. What if inactive members are people you really don't want back—that is, persistently troublemaking individuals who have repeatedly done serious injury to the congregation?

Q. When a persistent troublemaker has voluntarily inactivated membership in a church, is there any other response needed beyond a sigh of relief?

A. In another book I have defined a problem, not restricted to churches, but peculiarly destructive to them, as follows:

> Antagonists are individuals who, on the basis
> of non-substantive evidence, go out of their way

to make insatiable demands, usually attacking the person or performance of others. These attacks are selfish in nature, tearing down rather than building up, and are frequently directed against those in a leadership capacity. [3]

The existence of antagonism in churches creates a special circumstance when it comes to inactive members who are, or might be, antagonists. It also makes your questions difficult ones to answer because they are fraught with ethical overtones. Every congregation needs to address this issue for itself, very prayerfully and very carefully. There are some questions that can serve as guidelines.

- How long has the individual been behaving like this?
- Does the person's behavior tend to build up or tear down?
- How has that individual's behavior affected the overall ministry of the congregation, looking at effects on members and effects on outreach?
- How has the environment or atmosphere changed since the person left?
- If the person returns, are you willing to have the same conditions prevail?

If the individual in question is a true antagonist, the answers to these questions will suggest what course of action you should take. Sometimes the most caring and loving act—for everyone!—is to let someone go. You need to be concerned for the antagonist's soul, definitely, but there is more than one soul at stake here. Antagonists leave broken lives and spiritual destruction in their wake.

Q. How much do antagonists contribute to inactivity of others?

A. A significant amount—perhaps more than we know. When I conduct workshops on inactivity, there is a segment called "How Church Antagonism Causes Inactivity." After I talk about it briefly, and I have defined and described antagonistic conflict, I ask, "How many of you have ever seen this type of person in your congregation or some other congregation?" On a consistent basis about 75% raise their hands. Then I ask, "Of those of you who have seen antagonists, how many of you have seen their antagonism cause inactivity?" It's amazing. There is always a near-perfect correspondence, a one-to-one correlation. However many hands there were to the first question, there are almost the same number for the second question.

Sometimes people get fed up with unhealthy bickering that just seems to go on and on. They leave, and many times they view this as the healthy response to a sick situation. Conflict itself can be quite healthy, and by no means is most conflict caused by antagonists. But antagonistic conflict is sick. Here's the way one man describes it.

> A cousin of mine in the Midwest has been through a major church split within the past two years. It's significant that the antagonist who left behind so much bitterness and such a sense of powerlessness among the members of that congregation also did the same thing to another church a few years earlier. I anticipate he will do the same thing again to this new congregation that has arisen as a result of the split.

What makes people choose to become inactive is not only the presence of antagonists, but the fact that often nothing is done about them. This causes anxiety and a whole host of other emotions, including sadness, dejection, and frustration. Who wants to be part of an environment like that? Healthy people don't. The pastor, church leaders, and the whole congregation have an obligation to deal with this problem constructively and immediately.

Q. Are you recommending that I not take any action with

an inactive member who is an antagonist? Or should I at least visit the individual once?

A. Realize that my recommendations relate to visiting an antagonist *as an inactive member.* During actual antagonistic conflict, you may very well already have followed through with the prescriptions outlined in Matthew 18:15-17. If the individual is still spewing venom and it is likely that the Body of Christ will be injured, let go. Jesus let Judas go. Antagonists are not going to be very receptive to ministry. Do continue to pray for such individuals, for sure.

Q. Are you saying that everyone who criticizes is an antagonist?

A. By no means. In fact, most individuals who criticize are not antagonists. What is missing, among other characteristics, is the insatiable quality that drags problems out interminably. Antagonists are tremendously damaging individuals whose goals are very unhealthy. Most people who criticize want to build up rather than tear down. If their unhappiness has been properly contained, and they have not expressed this in ways damaging to the health of the overall congregation, do not just leave them alone. The responsible congregation needs to reach out to them, build a bridge to them, touch them, care for them, listen to them.

Notes

1 Ruth N. Koch and Kenneth C. Haugk, *Speaking the Truth in Love: How to Be an Assertive Christian* (St. Louis: Stephen Ministries, 1992).

2 Lyle E. Schaller, *Assimilating New Members* (Nashville, TN: Abingdon Press, 1978), pp. 74-77.

3 Kenneth C. Haugk, *Antagonists in the Church: How to Identify and Deal with Destructive Conflict* (Minneapolis: Augsburg, 1988), pp. 21-22.

8

Setting the Stage

Imagine that you are at home sitting in your favorite chair, and you are wondering whether or not to contact an inactive member. You have pretty much resolved to do it. This resolve may have come about because you have noticed the absence (or some other indicator) of someone, or it may be that you are a member of a group specifically charged with reaching out intentionally to inactive members. First, however, you need to consider what brought you to the point of thinking about contacting the person.

Q. Who should be the first person to contact an inactive member?

A. The one to make the first contact should be the noticing one, the person who first realizes that an individual is inactive. If you see the need, act. There is no reason to refer the inactive member's name to a committee or a church staff person.

The "noticing one" might be a friend, or it might be one who just happens to encounter the inactive member. Equally, it might be one who is part of an inactive member team established for making intentional contacts with inactive members. It could also be a church staff person.

The point is not so much who should be the first person, but that there indeed be a first person. Anyone is appropriate. Don't wait around until the right person comes along. You have met the right person and he or she is you.

Q. When is the appropriate time to approach an inactive member?

A. Now—as soon as possible.

You don't need to wait until the person has been gone a set amount of time. This *as soon as possible* prescription might even mean talking with individuals who are still relatively active, but who are giving off signals that they might become inactive.

If you are considering talking to someone who has been inactive for a long time, a kind of fatalism may settle upon you: "Having neglected this person so long, it's too late now to try anything." Wrong. Earlier is better than later, but later is better than never.

What Are You Trying to Accomplish?

There are three questions you might consider asking yourself as you consider contacting an inactive member, and the first is this: What are you trying to accomplish? The answer is this simple: You hope to set up a meeting that will be the beginning of a quality relationship with the inactive member.

Q. What is the best place to meet with inactive persons? In their homes? In my home? In a neutral setting such as a restaurant?

A. The place to seek is one where you can talk privately and where the inactive member feels the most comfortable.

There are potential advantages and disadvantages to each of the sites you mention.

In their own homes, inactive members are likely to feel most comfortable. It's the "home court advantage," and inactive members may appreciate the extra security this gives them. Always you want to minimize the natural defensiveness inactive members could feel, and the comfort of being on their own turf can help. There is also a subtle and desirable message in your willingness to come to them rather than expecting them to come to you. Possible disadvantages have to do with privacy. There may be small children or others present who provide a distraction from conversation in depth.

In your home, the advantages have to do with the hospitality you can show. The disadvantages are related to turf and privacy again. The inactive member may be more defensive when on your ground rather than his or hers. Likewise, if your home is not free from distractions or interruptions, the conversation will be much less likely to get beyond superficial pleasantries.

In a neutral place, you again have the opportunity to show hospitality, buying lunch for the individual for instance. Lacking other distraction-free options, a restaurant might be your only choice. If you work near one another, getting together for lunch may be a good way to make your two schedules coincide. A disadvantage, of course, is that public places are not the best for private conversations.

There are pluses and minuses to each of these alternatives. Your situation and the situation of the inactive member will guide your choice. All other things being equal, my preference generally is to meet in the inactive member's home. More often than not that will be the best alternative.

Q. How frequently should intentional, personal contacts take place with inactive members?

A. There is no absolute rule of thumb that will cover all situations. If your first meeting has been a good one, warm and relational, you will sense the inactive member's desire to talk more. In this situation you will not want to let a next get-together be delayed longer than a week, or two at the most. You might say, "Let's do this again. I think we've talked about a lot of good things, and I don't want to wait too long to get together again, if it's all the same to you." If you then see assent (a nod or other positive indicator), ask, "When do you think might be a good time?" or "What about next week?"

It's a good idea to set up the next visit before you say good-bye. Otherwise you run the risk of exchanging good intentions without ever solidifying them.

How Do You Proceed?

The second of the three questions for you to consider is: How do you proceed?

Q. How do you get in touch with an inactive member you don't already know, without its being a turnoff?

A. You do have a lot in common with the person, that's the first point for you to realize. You are both Christians. You belong to the same congregation.

Some congregations neglect inactive members because "no one knows them." The assumption seems to be that you have to have an already-established relationship in order to reach out to them, but that just isn't so.

Come across in the initial contact as warmly as possible. When outreach efforts have been turnoffs, it usually isn't because of the level of acquaintance of the people involved, but because of the cold or results-oriented way the active person came across.

Q. I've heard the suggestion that congregations do a phone survey of inactive members to listen to them and to show the congregation's interest. What do you think about this approach?

A. I know of many situations where this approach has

produced positive results. Simply the act of telephoning inactive members helps them to feel wanted, to feel that they are important.

The effectiveness of these calls does depend on how the caller comes across. If the message is simply a lecture about coming back to church, these calls will cause resentment, not communicate caring. If the calls are genuinely for listening and checking in, they tend to be received well.

The telephone can be used to reach out initially to inactive members, but the call must then be followed by one or more personal visits. Otherwise telephone contact just becomes another way of trying to do "cheap and easy ministry" with individuals who deserve far better.

Q. I've been talking with some people who have been ministering to inactive members a lot longer than I have, and they seem to be split on whether it is better to just drop by an inactive member's home unannounced, or to call ahead of time. Which is better?

A. Call first. It is not a matter of personal choice, but a necessity. There are several reasons and considerable research behind the positive certainty of my answer. Do so because . . .

- It shows your respect for the person's time and schedule.

- You want more than just a couple of minutes to talk to the person, which is all you may get if you drop by without warning. The person needs to carve out a specific chunk of time for your visit.

- You owe them time to prepare themselves for your visit. Individuals who are put on the spot by your unexpected visit may tell you what they think you want to hear—"I'll be in church next Sunday." If you have given the individual time to think, he or she is likely to be open and honest with you.

- You can be more certain of seeing everyone involved. In the case of married couples, their activity levels are often the same, so when one becomes inactive the spouse will often follow suit. Drop-in visits make it more likely you will miss one party or the other, or all.

- The telephone conversation itself can begin the process of bridge-building. If you conduct the phone call caringly, nonjudgmentally, and nonmanipulatively, chances are that the face-to-face meeting will get off to a good, positive start.

Q. I see what you're saying, but I drop by all the time without calling to set up an appointment, and it works fine. How do you explain that?

A. One explanation may be that the people you are visiting are being polite to you, but heaving a sigh of relief when you get out the door. Even if this is not the case, however, your advance call will signal to the inactive member your respect for him or her as an individual.

I surveyed more than 2,000 people on this matter, including formerly inactive members and always-active members. After describing the situation, I posed the question: Would they like to receive a call ahead of time? Eighty percent said they definitely would want a call, twenty percent said it made no difference. These odds are stacked against you. You run too much risk of getting off on the wrong foot if you don't call, four-to-one that the individual you drop by to see will be uncomfortable or offended.

Q. Doesn't calling people ahead of time to set up a visit give them too much of an opportunity to reject you?

A. The issue is one of control. The lives of inactive members have already assumed an out-of-control air to them. If you do not even offer the courtesy of an advance phone call, all you are doing is reinforcing their own feelings of impotence. This is the last thing you want to do.

Just seeing the inactive member is not what you are after. In fact, you are not "after" anything except the opportunity to relate to and care for the individual. That care begins with your respect and courtesy, which means it begins with the phone call you make to ask permission to visit.

Q. In setting up a visit, should you mention explicitly why you are calling? Should you mention the person's inactivity as the reason for your call?

A. The reason you are getting in touch with the individual is because you care and because you are full of the love of Jesus Christ. You want to contact that person in order to find out what is going on in his or her life. You are not calling about the person's inactivity; you are calling about the person him- or herself.

It is the individual's inactivity, however, that has created the occasion for the call. Certainly you can be open about that if it comes up, just don't belabor the point. Mention it and move on. You might say, for instance: "I'm calling to show care for you personally, not to get you back to church. But it is true that I would not be calling except for the fact that your absence was noted." Saying this will keep you from appearing to have a hidden agenda. Even if you never say it in so many words to the inactive member, recite it for yourself just as a reminder of the real reasons for your presence.

What If the Inactive
Member Says No?

The third question for you to consider ahead of time is this: What if the inactive member says no to your request for a visit?

Q. How do you work with individuals who don't want to be worked with?

A. Lower the intensity. Lower the threat. Lower the inactive member's defensiveness by avoiding the foot-in-mouth style of relating.

For a great number of inactive members who communicate that they do not want to be worked with, the real issue is that they do not want to be "worked over," which is what they have come to expect. When you relate to them differently—with love, care, listening, and empathy—most inactive members will be quite willing to risk developing a friendship with you.

Q. What if you call someone to set up a meeting and he or she simply refuses to meet with you?

A. Be persistent, though not pushy. Tell the person that you would really like to visit. If resistance continues, you may want to ask (in this call or a later one), "Do you think I'm coming over to give you a hard time about church involvement?" If the answer is yes, directly or indirectly, reassure the individual that such is not the purpose of your call: "I'm just calling to check in with you and find out how things are going with you. If you want to talk about the church, I would be happy to do so. But if you don't want to, that's fine too."

If you are clear and genuine in your expressions of concern, it is very likely that a fellow Christian would want you to visit. Be nonjudgmental, noncontrolling, open, honest, and respectful. By so doing, you will diminish the perceived threat.

Q. What if the refusal to meet with you is really firm?

A. Listen to what the individual is saying. If the person says, "I'm too busy" (which may or may not be the true reason), you can say, "That's okay. I'd like to check back with you later when things have slowed down." The individual might also be saying, "I really don't want to be part of this congregation any longer." Does the person want you to relay this back to the congregation?

Sometimes *no* means, "Coax me," but sometimes no means

no, too. If you have been persistent without being pushy and the individual continues to refuse to meet, back off for a while, but do try again later. If you've only been turned down once, I'd say try again in two or three weeks.

Q. How determined should one be in trying to "get with" an inactive member who has become inactive specifically because of an unfortunate encounter with an individual in the congregation? This inactive member steadfastly refuses to meet.

A. You should be very persistent with this person. Presumably you have examined your determination to "get with" the inactive member and have eliminated numbers, glory, money, full pews, and the like as motivations. Those are not good reasons for being persistent. If, however, your goal is to share God's love, to build up the Body of Christ, and to minister to that person, then you can be persistent with a clean heart. Having a "clean heart" makes a good subject for your prayerful entreaties:

> Create in me a clean heart, O God,
> and put a new and right spirit within me.
> Do not cast me away from your presence,
> and do not take your holy spirit from me.
> Restore to me the joy of your salvation,
> and sustain in me a willing spirit.
> Psalm 51:10-12

Q. Is there much difference between a pastor's and a lay person's exercise of persistence?

A. If there is, there is a problem. When you get right down to it, both are ministers equally charged with caring for brothers and sisters in the faith and in the world.

Q. What happens if you call an inactive member on the

phone and he or she refuses to meet face-to-face, but is willing to talk over the phone?

A. All things being equal, face-to-face encounters are definitely best. You lose a lot of information when you can't see the other person.

When you have no choice, do your best on the telephone. Here are some points adapted from the Stephen Series training module "Telecare: The Next Best Thing to Being There":

1. Listen carefully. You have to rely solely on what you pick up by sound.

2. Check out your assumptions periodically. Because you have only sound to rely on, you can't always be sure what's happening. (Example: "It's difficult for me to tell right now how you are feeling.")

3. Try for a "clean sound" environment. Don't talk with the radio or TV on. Use another room if there is distracting background noise in the room you are in.

4. Confirm your listening with verbal cues now and then, since the inactive member can't see you.

5. Be conscious of the tones of your voice. Communicate warmth and caring. Be clear, distinct in your responses. Make your voice lively rather than a monotone.

6. Ask yourself, "Whose needs am I satisfying?" Put aside your own needs and make every effort to address the needs of the inactive member.

7. Keep the conversation focused. You may have to bring the conversation away from chat and refocus on the purpose of your call, which is to offer care to the other and discover what his or her needs are. (Small talk can serve a kind of "testing-the-waters" purpose for the inactive member, however, so don't be too quick to steer the conversation back to the "important stuff." For the inactive member at that moment, the small talk may be the important stuff.)

8. When it's time to say good-bye, say it. If the inactive member starts to repeat, or seems to fumble for what

to say next, end the phone call appropriately. Indicate your intention of calling back to check in, and be sure you follow up on that intention. You certainly ought to offer once again to meet.

Q. How do you deal with your own feelings if you get turned down when you call to set up a visit?

A. Certainly there are no easy solutions, but there are a number of possibilities for you to consider.

First, realize you cannot control others no matter how hard you try or how good your intentions are. Others are in charge of their own lives, not you.

Second, pray about the situation and the individual. Offer your attempt to God, and your feelings of rejection too. In your prayer, apologize for your shortcomings, known and unknown. Praise God in the certainty that his will for you and the inactive individual is for the well-being of both of you.

Third, check your own motivations. If you have truly attempted to set up a visit with good intentions, to offer care and with a desire to find out what is going on with the inactive member rather than intending to haul him or her back to church, you are perfectly justified in considering your effort as honorable. You've lived up to God's hopes for you.

Fourth, recognize that you are a "person-in-process," not perfect yet, though God's working on it! As you become more skilled through training and experience, you will do better at reaching out to others. You will become more aware of the importance of getting your own house in order, so that the motivations you have, which affect the way you come across, are the right ones.

Note

Adapted with permission from "Telecare: The Next Best Thing to Being There," *Stephen Series Leader's Manual* (St. Louis: Stephen Ministries, 2000).

9

Reaching Out

You are setting forth on high adventure when you reach out to an inactive member. This is a child of God you relate to, a person within whom you will encounter none other than Jesus Christ, for so he has promised in Matthew 25:40: "Truly I tell you, just as you did it to one of the least of these who are members of my family, you did it to me."

As if those rewards were not enough, you also have the prospect before you of making a new friend. The inactive member is full of newness, and you are privileged to explore that landscape. But what can you expect as you first reach out? That is the substance of the questions in this chapter.

Q. Is it better to visit as one person or as a team?

A. One person is better than two. The message, when two people show up on a doorstep, is too easily read as, "We're here to out-vote, out-flank, out-think, and out-weigh you." You are there to develop a relationship, and relationships are more likely to be diluted in two-on-one situations.

Your primary aim is to not threaten the inactive member,

who is very likely feeling threatened already because of the impending visit. Realize that two of you showing up would double the threat.

Q. If I go solo, how do I deal with my own fear and apprehension in my earliest visits?

A. Training in the proper skills will do much to relieve your anxiety. In training you ought to be exposed to enough practice role plays and simulated experiences to give you a pretty good idea what to expect on a visit. The relief from a results-oriented approach, which also ought to be emphasized during training, will certainly free you from some fears you anticipate now.

In Chapter 5 you have already read that I strongly endorse matching gender of callers to inactive members—men calling on men, women on women. If you arrive at a home expecting a couple to be waiting for you and only the party of the opposite sex is present, then use your own judgment about proceeding. If you pick up any indication of hazard, my recommendation would be to wait and try again later.

Q. What should I do if I set up a time to meet with an inactive member and he or she is not home when I arrive?

A. Instances of this actually occurring are, as Mark Twain said about rumors of his death, "greatly exaggerated." Don't let this possibility worry you too much. And if it does happen, don't assume the worst, that the individuals are avoiding you. In all likelihood they are not. They might have just gotten busy and forgotten you were coming, or perhaps some emergency arose.

Be positive. Most inactive members want someone to respond to their "cry for help." The best course of action for you in the event this does occur is to leave a note saying, "Sorry I missed you." Call the individual a day or so later to set up another time for a visit.

Q. I've heard that it takes a minimum of five visits before one gets a response from an inactive member. Is this true?

Q. I've heard it said that one visit is necessary for each year of inactivity. Do you agree?

A. One visit will get a response if it is a visit in which you genuinely express caring, openness, and a willingness to listen. The Christ in the other reaches out to the Christ in you.

Watch out for the results-oriented thinking these questions provoke. "Well, I'll try one more visit (or two more, or whatever), and then I'll quit calling on this person." What these two questioners are probably asking is, "How many visits are necessary before an inactive member returns to church?" This last question presumes to know already the proper response for the inactive person—returning to church. While I certainly hope for the inactive member's return, I don't set that up as a precondition for visiting.

The questions to ask yourself are these: Is a quality relationship developing? Is ministry going on? As long as the answer is yes, keep on keeping on. If you are part of an inactive member group—those charged with intentionally reaching out to inactive members—the ongoing team meetings you attend can help you examine these latter questions. If you are acting on your own, consider the development of your relationship with the inactive member as best you can.

Q. What about reaching out to someone in response to news that this person is going to another church?

A. Look into your own motivation first. With the right motivation—to care and to learn—making such a visit is very sensible. With the wrong motivation—simply to try to make a case for the individual's return to your church—such a visit would be the worst thing you could do, terribly out of place.

There is a high probability that this individual will not be returning to your church. Why visit, then? The church can learn from the business world here. For many businesses, when an employee leaves for whatever reason, a supervisor conducts an "exit interview." The business expects to, and often does, learn much about what it is doing right and wrong in such an interview.

There is much for a congregation to learn from a member who is leaving or has left already. Is something awry in the congregation? Is there something the congregation could do better that would make this less likely to happen in the future? Express to the person your honest interest and need to know what his or her feelings and thoughts are about all this. Express your gratitude for whatever bits of information the person is gracious enough to share. You are likely to be learning ways that will help make your congregation more like a home for present and future members.

Maybe the person is just testing the waters, too. Attendance at another church can be a person's way of sending out a "cry for help," a plea for someone to relate to him or her. If so, you will soon find that out when you express an interest in visiting the individual. If not, if the individual is happy in a new church affiliation, you can celebrate that fact and bestow a blessing on him or her.

Q. How do you approach persons or a family inactive for five years, or ten years, but who still consider themselves members of the church?

A. Call them. Say, "How are things going?" Say, "I called because I hoped I could come by for a visit." Don't make it a big deal, with drums rolling in the background. Listen, love, and care.

Many times a new pastor, for example, can do wonders by saying, "I'm new to the congregation, and I am calling on all who are on the membership list. I'd like to visit with you."

The inactive member may say in so many words, or by implication, "Are you after me to get me back to church?"

Then the pastor or lay person can assure the inactive member, "No, I just want to get to know you better." Why can you offer that reassurance? Because that's what you sincerely do want. You are not just trying to get a foot in the door so you can launch into a sales pitch. I hope by this point in this book you are getting the idea that relating to people with ulterior motives sounds a death-knell to any real relationship developing, and also woefully diminishes the likelihood of an individual's return.

Q. How long should a visit be with an inactive member?

A. An hour is a good average to keep in mind. The visit could go longer, perhaps an hour and a half or so, if you and the inactive member get involved in a very extensive discussion. The time needs to be long enough for significant sharing to take place.

Don't overstay your welcome. One way you can gauge that length is by who is doing most of the talking. If it's the inactive member doing most of the talking, that's a good sign. Tend to stay longer. If it's you doing most of the talking, cut it short and leave.

If your visit has its roots in results-oriented thinking, make it as short as possible. Better yet, don't make such a visit at all. Even five minutes of results-oriented bombast is too much. If you are there to try to argue the person back to church, you shouldn't be there.

Q. What do you talk about with an inactive member?

A. Whatever the inactive member wants to talk about.

Q. In relating to an inactive member, when do you finally turn the inactive member over to God, finally "let go and let God?"

A. Do so from the beginning. Surrendering of the illusion of control is the real beginning of process-oriented ministry. It is a huge misconception to think that it's all right for you to "have control" of the situation until the going gets really tough, and then you can "let go and let God." You do not ever have control of the situation. You do not ever have control of the inactive member. Fortunately for you and everyone concerned, God does.

Q. Would you speak to the value of allowing the inactive member to "dump" on the caller? Is it necessary and worthwhile to allow this?

A. I assume that by *dump* you mean allowing and encouraging the inactive member to unburden him- or herself of quite strong feelings, including anger and hurt. It is necessary, which doesn't mean it's pleasant for you.

But worthwhile ministry includes the Apostle Paul's charge to "bear one another's burdens" (Gal. 6:2), and in one sense you should jump for joy when an inactive member trusts you enough to share feelings honestly. It shows that the individual still cares about the church, for if the inactive member did not care, no ventilation, no dumping, would take place.

This does not change the fact that it isn't easy, and at times it may be painful for you. But the growth for you and the inactive member both makes it worthwhile. Here's what one individual said:

> I have learned so much by listening to hurting, angry inactive members. I get to know so much about their inner values and feelings, and when I've let them dump anger, they've often gone on later to share really startling hurts.
>
> Another point is that their dumping gives me another perspective of the congregation. What they say often stimulates thinking that leads to some really good ideas for how to make God's house more like a home.

My own growth has been helped too. Ministering to angry inactive persons has taught me how to deal with other situations where there are differences and disagreements. I can deal with conflict in much healthier and more effective ways now.

In the process of healing that must take place, dumping can also be the precursor to genuine confession and repentance on the part of the inactive member. This may take place with you, with another, or internally in a dialogue with God. (This is by no means to suggest that everything that "ails" most inactive members is something requiring confession and repentance on their part.) In a nutshell, the value of dumping is that it can be the beginning of healing.

Q. How can I avoid making things worse as I talk with inactive members?

A. Here are some practical tips for you:

1. Keep tuned in to how much talking you are doing. You should definitely talk much less than the inactive member. More than one-fourth of the time is probably too much talking by you.
2. Listen with all the skill at your command.
3. Care with your whole heart for the inactive individual.
4. Be patient.
5. Be genuine.
6. Throw out any preset agenda you have. You are there to learn the inactive member's needs, not to prescribe solutions.

Q. Inactive members I visit are sometimes wary of me

because I am an active member in the congregation. How can I reduce those initial barriers?

A. First, pray. Pray for yourself, that God would give you the strength, patience, understanding, and ability to endure. Pray to be nonmanipulative and nonjudgmental. Thank God, who is already present in the inactive member, for creating an openness to what you say.

Second, search your motives and attitudes. No need to repeat here what I've already said at length elsewhere.

Third, relate caringly when you are with the inactive member. You do not need to hurdle barriers, crash through them, or melt them. You simply need to be the embodiment of Christ, and that is not as difficult as you might think because the promise is already there for you: You are the embodiment of Christ!

Q. What can I do to help inactive members see their personal need for God?

A. This question brings out the Socratic in me: What makes you think you have to do anything extra to help inactive members see their personal need for God? Who says they don't see it already, without your help?

You must go into a relationship with inactive members without arrogance, and arrogance is very much in evidence if one comes across sounding like, "I have a strong faith and these inactive members have a weak faith. My role is to help them shore up their weak faith so that they come back to church."

Lack of faith or an inability to see a personal need for God is not all that often the cause of inactivity. Research bears this out. When asked, most inactive members espouse quite a deep faith in God and do recognize their need for corporate worship. But something else is going on that makes them choose absence. To talk with them about their personal need for God will almost certainly miss the mark altogether.

Q. Since a person's spiritual welfare is of concern, when in the conversation might you raise questions about that person's relationship to God?

A. Be very careful in taking this line. One possibility is not to raise such questions at all, or rarely, although I realize the radical nature of this answer. The benefits of such a line of questioning would be minimal, and the potential for harm to the developing relationship would be great. Remember that a person's relationship with God, or lack of it, is hardly ever the cause of inactivity.

What I suggest is that you wait until inactive members themselves bring up the subject, with the near-certainty they will do just that. Then by all means pick up the cue and talk about it. Their bringing up their relationship with God shows their readiness to talk about it. If you try to force it into the conversation, you will probably do more harm than good.

Q. What about the church or church attendance—when should you bring those subjects up?

A. Rarely, if ever. The inactive member will undoubtedly bring it up if you wait. The very fact of your presence is all the reminder the inactive person needs. Essentially the subject is brought up just by your being there, so trust the process and be patient. You won't have to wait long.

This recommendation worries many would-be visitors to inactive members. "Don't you care about the person's church attendance?" they ask. Yes, I do. I care so much that I'm not going to push for it. I know that as a result of my caring for the inactive member as a person, he or she is much more likely to return to church.

Inviting by your presence might not work in those instances where you and the inactive member already know each other— you're related, say, or friends. The existing relationship could screen off any connections in the inactive member's mind between you and church. In instances such as these, you certainly can bring up the subject of church, although I still wouldn't push, or rush the subject into your conversation.

Q. What should I say in chance meetings with inactive members?

A. I think people blow out of proportion the "task" of relating to inactive members in chance meetings. All you need do is relate naturally, as you would with a friend. What do you say to friends? Probably, "Hi, how are you?" "It's good to see you." "How are you doing?"

What you don't want to say is, "We miss you" or "Where have you been hiding?" or "It's good to see you're still alive." Most of the time statements like these will not go over well. The inactive person will likely (and rightly) get defensive.

The inactive person may already be feeling embarrassed by this meeting. Don't do anything that will make him or her feel more embarrassed. Do be warm and friendly, without making the individual feel cornered by your efforts at an extended conversation.

A chance meeting may be over and done with in a moment or two. This is not the time or the place to carry on deep conversations about highly personal matters. Don't even bring up the subject of church yourself. If the other person mentions it, say something like, "I'd really like to talk to you more about that, but I don't think this is the best place to do it. How about if we get together and catch up?" If you don't get a chance to make an arrangement there and then, use the meeting as a reason for calling later on.

Q. I've had these chance meetings you talk about, and I've always tried to make it a point to be friendly and chat for a bit. But it never seems to pay off. What am I doing wrong?

A. Just keep on doing what you are doing. You need to leave some things to God. When you worry too much about the payoff—and I assume you mean having the person return to church—you are really usurping a role that rightfully belongs to God. One goal of a chance encounter is that you not do anything that will cause the person to be even more estranged from the church. Another goal is that you simply share love and care in that moment in time.

Why do you care? At the deepest level, as a Christian, it is because you are redeemed by Christ and are therefore able to share his love with others. Your care is not contingent upon a certain response from the inactive member. It is based on who you are, not what he or she does.

Q. As a pastor of a congregation, in chance encounters with inactive members I find it very difficult just to offer warm and friendly greetings. Even though I know by experience it's counterproductive, I still find myself tempted to "go for them" when I meet them. What can I do to bring these unruly impulses under control?

A. Your knowledge of the uselessness of trying to browbeat someone into returning to church is a good start. Keep telling yourself that, because you are 100% correct. In addition, I suggest prayer. Try biting your tongue, too.

To the best of your ability, put yourself in the other's shoes. How would you want to be treated if the tables were turned? You'd want to be treated with friendliness. You certainly would not want your pastor to be aloof and avoid you, but neither would you want to be pressured. What you would probably hope for is a kind, friendly, and perhaps a reasonably brief encounter, with no hint of haughtiness, superiority, manipulation, or judgment on the part of the pastor.

You can manage all that, because you already have the knowledge, and knowledge affects actions if you permit it to.

10

Breaking the Ice and Getting Past Hello

Your first visit with an inactive member may have all the elements of a good story. There may be a beginning, middle, and end, and character development of the principals in the story—you and the inactive member. If the story is a satisfying one, there may also be the signs of a relationship beginning to develop, which makes the story of that first visit even more like the first chapter in a novel.

What to Do at the Beginning

Q. Do you have any suggestions on how to begin a conversation or visit with an inactive member?

A. I think people need to lower their anxiety level considerably and look at conversations with inactive individuals as just an interaction between two human beings. This is not a meeting between an "active" person and an "inactive" person, but between Laura and Amy, or Andrew and Nathan—between two people with names, in other words. My first suggestion, therefore, is to relax.

Mostly, anxiety about a first visit is related to having a results orientation. There is also the normal anxiety that goes with any first-time meeting. You have learned the futility of a results orientation, so you should be freed from that burden. As to the shyness or tentativeness you may be feeling, just be as natural as you can. Talk with the inactive member in the same way you would anyone else.

The basic staples of greeting are yours to make use of: "Hi. How are you?" Because this phrase is so routine, maybe a little better would be, "How are things going with you?" or "How is life treating you?" Certainly you can add, "It's good to see you," or "It's good to meet you."

Q. What do you say after you say hello?

A. Again, you don't need to make a big deal of this. Simply be genuine. Be casual. If the person is a stranger to you, you would spend some time getting acquainted. If you know the person already, less time would be necessary.

I'm going to give you guidelines rather than a canned speech. Formulas for relationships are self-defeating. You feel unnatural. The other individual hears the artificiality and feels unnatural, too. You are just two people getting to know one another.

The safest course is to focus on the other individual, having him or her bring you up to date on what's been going on. You have to be careful of making remarks such as "I've missed you." Share it only if and when it's definitely true, but recognize that a statement such as this can come across lacking genuineness and trigger defensive feelings in an inactive member, which you do not want to do. Get the other person to talk about him- or herself. Don't throw the church bulletin in the person's face, or a newsletter. Don't just "happen" to have their box of contribution envelopes with you. Don't come in with a planned agenda. You want to know what the other's needs are.

Q. If an inactive member responds to my greeting by complaining that the church is always asking for money, and that people are always contacting him or her for that reason, how do I respond?

A. The first thing you need to communicate, in no uncertain terms, is that money is *not* the reason you are visiting the person. (And that had better be true! Money is a totally inappropriate subject to be talking about to inactive members.) You could say, for example, "This might have been true other times, but I can promise you I'm not here to talk about money. As I mentioned on the phone, I just want to check in with you and see how things are going for you."

Will the inactive member believe you? Maybe, maybe not. That statement at least provides a measuring stick for the person to use as the conversation progresses. Trust will unfold as he or she sees the extent to which you live up to what you say.

What Not to Do

Q. As a way to break the ice and get the conversation going, should I first ask the inactive member why he or she became inactive, and then get into a discussion of that?

A. That is the exact opposite of what you should do. Starting there would be meeting your needs, not looking to the needs of the inactive member. Your focus has to be on the other's needs.

If you met someone with a bad sunburn, would your opening remark be, "So how's the old sunburn?" accompanied by a hearty smack on the back? If a family member who hasn't been home for three Christmases suddenly shows up, are you going to kick the conversation off by asking, "How come you haven't been home before this?" Both these openings would be rude and inconsiderate, and your native tactfulness already has told you that. First build a relationship of trust, then you will have earned the right to be shared with, and the inactive member will more than likely signal it by sharing with you spontaneously.

Q. Is too much zeal a danger in relating to inactive members?

A. As a matter of fact, I think anyone who reaches out to inactive members needs to have a very high degree of zeal. But the zeal has to be expressed in an accepting and loving way. Therein lies the answer to your question: The amount of zeal isn't the issue, but how it's channeled and what form it takes is.

Here's an example someone shared with me, in which misplaced zeal brought unfortunate consequences:

> One inactive woman in our congregation had been recently divorced, so I sent her a postcard telling her about the next meeting of a singles' support group that I headed. This was a case of being too full of my own agenda. From my vantage point, knowing how positive and supportive the group was, I couldn't imagine anyone taking such an invitation amiss. But from her point of view (as reported to me by another member of the singles group), "The church couldn't even wait until the ashes of my marriage were cold to try to get its hands on me!"
>
> My goof taught me two lessons. First, there is no substitute for personal contact. Second, I will never again offer my solutions for someone else's problems. Instead, I will spend some time listening to find out what his or her needs are.

Being careful about how you channel your zeal does not mean being apathetic, or totally letting the other person alone. Be zealous about caring. Be zealous about sharing Christ's love.

Real care is not overpowering. If you confine yourself to listening and being actively present with the other, you will already have the safeguards you need built into the relationship. This will require patience and self-restraint on your part, especially if you have previously thought of inactive members as individuals in the grip of apathy who need a strong shove to get them going again.

Q. Why does saying "I'll pray for you" seem to hit inactive members the wrong way?

A. First of all, when an active member says, "I'll pray for you" to an inactive member, this can communicate a lofty air of spiritual superiority. It may be interpreted by the inactive member as, "You poor, depraved individual, you need a lot of help and I am in a position to offer it to you because I have the inside track with God." A healthy response on the inactive member's part could be to look the active member square in the eye and reply, "And I'll pray for you, too!"

A second problem is that such words can seem to dismiss whatever the real needs of the inactive member are. *I'll pray for you* sounds glib in many contexts. It sounds like the person who says these words is looking for a quick and easy way to dispatch the other individual's problems, without taking the time to listen, to empathize, to get involved. Such a perception of you can be deadly to any relationship you would like to develop.

Finally, these words can be uncaring and manipulative, an attempt to bend the other to your will for him or her. Suppose an inactive member makes some critical statements about the congregation. To respond, "I'll pray for you" might very well be taken to mean, "I'll pray that you realize God wants you to quit complaining and get back to church." That's akin to the kind of prayer a church welcomer made for a new member who happened to be an excellent tenor, but wanted to serve as an usher. The choir needed tenors, so the welcomer closed his visit with this prayer: "Lord, please open Jim's heart and lead him to do his part where the congregation needs him most. Enable Jim's ministry, wherever he serves, to be like music in your ears!" A prayer like that may make newly active Jim become inactive Jim!

By the way, please do pray for the inactive member. You don't have to announce it at all, and in fact to do so could put you in league with the Pharisee who prayed publicly so all would see what a righteous fellow he was (Luke 18:10-12). But praying privately, in your inner room as Jesus suggests (Matt. 6:6), will be good for both you and the inactive member. It will be good for you because it reminds you that God is really the one who is at work in the inactive member's life. It is good for the inactive member because Scripture tells us it is (1 Tim. 2:1, 3-4).

There is a time when offering to pray with or for an inactive member is very appropriate. When the inactive member is dealing with an explicit life struggle, and the two of you have been talking about it, an offer to pray for the other is perfectly suitable. Suppose there has been a death in the family, for instance, or the inactive member has some major illness. Then to say, "I'll pray for you," shows your concern for the other, and will not be taken as an attempt to browbeat or cajole him or her. The difference is that you took the time to listen first, so that you really understood what the other was struggling with, and demonstrated your understanding during this sharing.

What to Do in the
Middle of the Visit

Q. In visiting inactive members, how do you keep the visit from being just a social call? How do you move to in-depth discussion?

A. The best way to move to in-depth sharing is to keep your mouth closed and your ears open. Inactive members and most everyone else will talk about all kinds of in-depth issues when they are ready. You have to respect their willingness and their sense of timing.

Keep the focus on feelings. Ask open-ended questions, which are questions that can't be answered yes or no. *How* and *what* are markers that indicate these kinds of questions.

Remember also that if you try to yank inactive members along to in-depth issues of your choosing, you risk never finding out what the issues are that really concern them. Many times when you think you know what's bothering an inactive member, in all probability you don't. The only way you will find out is by waiting and listening. Inactive members in many instances are struggling, sometimes crying out for help. They are just waiting for someone to come along who seems willing to listen. You can be that person.

Q. You said before that it's bad form to open up the conversation with a question about why the individual hasn't been involved. Should I ever ask an inactive member point-blank what his or her feelings are about the church?

A. Certainly, within the context of a relationship you can ask a question like that. The relationship will take more than one visit to develop, probably, so you would not be likely to ask such a question in a first visit. The chances are very high that the inactive member will bring up the subject him- or herself if you just wait. At that point you will be able to ask follow-up questions very naturally because you will base the questions on what the inactive member said.

Here's a powerful follow-up question you might ask the individual in the course of time: "Where have we failed you?" Or if this is a bit strong for you, phrase it: "Where might we have failed you?" To ask a question like this requires courage. Words such as these are not for the faint-hearted. But they are words that mark genuine, courageous care.

Q. If I think an inactive person is not telling the truth, how can I encourage more honesty?

A. Defensiveness on the part of the inactive member is not the equivalent of dishonesty. You can expect defensiveness, and honor it by taking seriously whatever the inactive member says. Respect his or her right to work up to letting you in on what he or she is thinking and feeling after some testing to see if you are trustworthy.

You work on trust in the relationship by being trustworthy yourself. Listen for the inactive member's feelings. Try not to get defensive. Keep your promises. In short, make yourself worthy of their honesty and then hope for the best.

Q. Suppose I believe an inactive member is just telling me what he or she thinks I want to hear—what do I do then?

A. Clarify what you want the individual to do. You could say, "I have an idea you're just telling me what you think I want to hear. But I am here to be honest with you, and I hope you will be honest with me." Tell the individual you want to know what is genuinely of concern to him or her. If you say, "I really do not have any preconceived ideas of what is best for you, and I'm not looking for some painted-over, sugary niceness, I just want to hear what is the truth," then most people will tell you the truth.

Now, how can you be convincing in saying this? Let that statement be a true reflection of your inner attitude. You can encourage the inactive member to be either insincere or genuine. If you see your role as simply being there to issue an invitation to come back to church, for example, then the inactive member will pick up on that and may try to get rid of you in a hurry by saying, "I'll be in church on Sunday." If you flinch, glare, breathe heavily, or clench your teeth when the inactive member gives an honest appraisal of some shortcomings of the church, the person will start to back away from further honesty. If you start trying to explain away some hurt the inactive member has experienced by offering a rationale for why it happened, the person is likely to back away. Mostly you want to listen and empathize, which means being actively present with the other while he or she states concerns and explains feelings.

Q. After a first visit, I thought there was a pretty good chance I had messed things up. I think I did everything wrong. The inactive member ended up being extremely negative and defensive. Is there anything I can do after the fact to retrieve the situation?

A. You can get back to the inactive member as soon as possible after the visit, saying some variation of the following:

"When we were talking the other day, I'm afraid I really came on like Mr. Know-it-all. I certainly wasn't listening very well to what you were trying to say. I was probably coming in with my own agenda, instead of being there with the purpose of hearing what you had to say. But what you have to say is what is important, and I feel embarrassed about the way I acted. I'm sorry."

Depending on the person's response, you might add:

"I sure hope we can talk again."

An honest apology to anyone, inactive or active, is one of the most powerful statements you can ever make. It's not easy to do, but it communicates care and concern for the other person's feelings in a way that hardly any other statement can. By being willing to admit your faults, you give the inactive member a chance to reconsider his or her decision to write you off. Your honesty and vulnerability may not retrieve the situation, but it's your only hope.

Q. Let's say we in our congregation start with reaching out to recently inactive members, but after a time we want to include those who have been inactive for more significant lengths of time. How can we go about relating to them?

A. Call them. Tell them you want to stop by and talk with them. The dialogue might go like this:

Inactive member: You're too late. I'm busy with other things now.
Active member: I'm really sorry we have let things go so long.

How will the individual respond to that? Probably he or she will be pleased. You might then say:

Active member: I'd still like to stop by.

Much of the time the person will agree to see you. But sometimes the dialogue might continue like this:

Inactive member: You're wasting your time—I'm not coming back to church.

Active member: I'm not calling to get you to come back to church. I'm calling because it's been a long time and I'd just like to sit down and talk with you. [Silence greets this assertion.] Do you believe me?

Inactive member: No, I don't.

Active member: I'll make a promise to you. If and when we get together, I'm not going to bring up church. If you want to, fine, but I won't bring it up. That's my commitment to you.

People will respond very positively to such openness on your part. You can be nearly certain they will bring up the subject of church, but if they don't, there will be plenty else to talk about that will tell you what their needs are.

Q. What is the single most effective way to attract an inactive member into wanting to be a more active part of a congregation?

A. Come across to the person in a caring, nonpossessive way, without trying to control or get results, but genuinely offering Christ's love to him or her.

This question is almost like asking, "How do I get someone to love me?" Perhaps the only possibility is to love the other person. There is very little you can do or say that will make another love you. It just won't happen. The only way an inactive member will regain love for a congregation is by being loved without conditions, as he or she is.

Q. If you had an opportunity to say just a few words to an inactive member, what would they be?

A. The exact words would vary depending on the situation and the individual to whom I was talking, as well as how I was feeling myself, but the gist of them would be:

"Tell me how things have been going with you."

From there on, my responses would depend entirely on what the individual said in reply.

Are you surprised? Perhaps you expected me to say something like:

- "I wish you would come back to church."
- "Please come back to church for your sake, for the congregation's sake, for God's sake."
- "We are concerned about you, your spirituality, your relationship with God."
- "God loves you so much. I wish you would realize that."

By this time in this chapter, I hope you are not surprised. I hope you realize that what inactive members need most from us is permission for them to share their concerns, and the listening ear to appreciate and respond to those concerns. By this time I hope you realize that you are to be the incarnation of Jesus, that same Jesus who paused to ask (Luke 18:41) the blind man of Jericho, "What do you want me to do for you?" Just as Jesus did not take for granted what the blind man would want, so it will be with you in ministry to inactive members. What is really important? Not what you say, but what the inactive member says.

11

How to Face Defensiveness and Criticisms

Every relationship with an inactive member will be unique, a fusion of your uniqueness and that of the person you are relating to. Despite that opening qualifier, this chapter is intended to give you a glimpse of the possibilities that might arise in your relationships, especially some of the more difficult possibilities. As is true of any relationship, when you are reaching out to an inactive member you may meet some situations that require you to be on the alert and informed. The first of these is . . .

Defensiveness

Q. What if the inactive member I'm talking with will not give any reason for inactivity, or says there is no particular reason?

A. Most of the time when individuals do not share reasons, or the reasons they give are not credible, it is because they are wary of anticipated judgment, argument, or cajolery. That wariness is just another name for defensiveness.

Confronted with such wariness, one response for you is to examine how you are coming across. Are you demanding to know reasons? Do your questions have an edge to them, perhaps because you are harboring some judgmentalism?

The other counsel I have is for patience. Continue to be honest, calm, caring, and accepting over the course of several visits and you will undoubtedly see the defensiveness begin to melt away as the other starts to trust that you really mean what you say. You really aren't there to judge. You really do care.

A note of caution here, too: You may be amazed at the details people will share, but watch your reactions when the inactive member does begin to share at a more personal level. Obvious shock or surprise on your part, for example, would be certain to send the inactive member scurrying back into defensive behavior.

Q. What if I am dealing with someone who is extremely defensive?

A. Don't make any sudden moves. Maybe you think I'm joking, but I'm not. The relationship between you and an inactive member is loaded with potential for defensiveness. Be as gentle and as gingerly as you would be with a squirrel in the park that you were trying to entice to take a nut from your fingers.

Inactive members have defensive reactions when they perceive that the active member is:[1]

- evaluating them;
- attempting to control them;
- operating from more than one motivation, or from ambiguous motivation;
- being dishonest by pretending to be neutral;
- giving an impression of being superior; and
- acting certain of the rightness of his or her cause.

Equipped as you are with a process-oriented approach to inactive members rather than a results-oriented approach, you will be sheltered from many mistakes. A results-oriented approach increases defensiveness; a process-oriented approach diminishes it.

Nevertheless, you are bound to run into defensiveness, and you should be prepared for it ahead of time. Watch out for your own tendencies to get defensive in the face of defensiveness. That's a common reaction, but it won't do your relationship with the inactive member any good. Be conscious of the messages you are communicating, both verbally and nonverbally.

Criticisms

Q. How can I respond to a very realistic criticism of the congregation—one that might be justified—without disparaging my congregation, the staff, or lay leaders?

A. You have correctly recognized the prickly nature of this sort of situation, which requires careful handling. Exchanges such as this are likely to occur not only in interactions between inactive and active members, but also between two active members. So what do you do?

Oftentimes all the person who is criticizing needs is a sense that his or her criticism is being heard. You do not have to defend or rush to agree with the person. Your primary role is as a listener. Simply reflect what you hear to make sure you have it right and to verify for the inactive member that you understand. Then you might say, "I understand what you are saying, and I appreciate your comments. I will look into this matter and see what can be done to improve the situation or avoid this in the future. I'll get back to you."

Be sure you follow through. Do take the criticism back, do make sure the matter is discussed, and do get back to the inactive member.

Whatever you do, don't try to sweep the criticism under the rug or smooth the matter over. If you seem mainly interested in dismissing the criticism, the inactive member will feel like you are trivializing whatever he or she said. Don't hasten to suggest that the inactive member should forgive and forget— that would make it seem as though the problem were only the inactive member's.

In some ways, you can welcome such criticisms. The fact

that the inactive member shares them with you shows that you have proved yourself worthy of trust. Besides, this kind of feedback can be a very positive challenge to the congregation for improvement.

Situations like this will not occur as much if the leadership and church staff have taken steps to ensure open communications ahead of time, which is a great way to prevent inactivity. When changes are taking place, good communication prepares the way for those changes; bad communication or none at all makes the changes disruptive.

Q. What if I take the criticism back to the leaders, and they really don't want to do anything about whatever the subject of the criticism is?

A. Resistance to some change is not always a negative. Make sure you understand the why behind the leaders' resistance. Very good, realistic reasons can exist for not making some changes. The criticism may not be justified. You need to understand clearly so you can explain adequately to the inactive member.

Depending on what the leadership says, you may need to suggest—assertively, not aggressively—more open-mindedness on the leaders' part, especially if the criticism is a recurrent one held by a number of individuals. Lay the whole situation out as completely as possible for the leaders. Give them information to help in their decision making. Be prepared to explain it—patiently—more than once if necessary.

Aggressive behavior will work no more with leadership than it would with inactive members. Aggression alienates people and creates barriers of defensiveness. Your case will benefit if you are caring in your assertiveness.

Q. If the inactive member is saying, "I'll be back when we have a new pastor," what response should I make?

A. The classic response to this statement is a lecture to individuals about how the pastor should not be the primary focus in their faith. The lecturer usually continues with observations about the need for commitment to Jesus Christ and to the congregation as the earthly community of believers. Lectures like this are rarely effective, if ever.

Instead, a level-headed member of the congregation should sit down with the inactive member and listen. I say "level-headed" because this person is undoubtedly going to hear some negatives about the pastor. The person therefore will need to be accepting and nonargumentative without seeming to endorse everything the inactive member is saying. The listener might say right at the beginning, "I'm not here to become part of a 'pastor-bashing' alliance. I'm just here to listen to you because what you say is important."

Then the person just listens. Follow up with that person. After the inactive member has been thoroughly heard out, then and only then the listener might choose to clarify some points.

The goal of all this listening is not to get the inactive member back to church, which may or may not be appropriate. One aim is to let the person get feelings out in the fresh air, get festering complaints off his or her chest. The main hope is that the person realizes he or she is cared for.

Pastors in particular may feel uncomfortable with providing such a forum for complainers, feeling that it gives people an unwarranted opportunity to slur the pastor's reputation. I don't want to burst any bubbles, but if someone (inactive or otherwise) is feeling reproachful, the pastor will be criticized anyway! Overall, giving someone an opportunity to share feelings in a structured, one-on-one setting can only be positive—for the inactive member, for the congregation, and yes, for the pastor as well.

One caution, however: If the individual is an antagonist according to the definition I shared in Chapter 7, none of this applies. To give such individuals a hearing will only serve to inflame their destructive impulses further.

Q. We have a situation in our congregation in which both active and inactive members are saying the pastor is not a good preacher. What can we do about this? My own view is that his preaching is not terrific, but he has other abilities that much more than compensate for his lackluster sermons.

A. Assuming that you have verified this perception with others, particularly those who are not chronic complainers, then the sermon-delivery difficulty is relatively straightforward to address. Have one or two individuals who are close to the pastor sit down with him or her and very lovingly communicate the problem. This is not a prescription for browbeating, bullying, or witch-hunting. You are not licensing the "strongest" members of the congregation to barge in to "straighten the pastor out." Presuming the pastor accepts this feedback as legitimate, the next concern is what to do about it. There are several options, helpful individually and in combination.

1. Encourage your pastor to check on when and where workshops and preaching clinics are being held. Provide money (it should already be available in a budget item for continuing education for your pastor anyway) and ask the pastor to attend.

2. Find out when the advanced or follow-up clinic is going to be held, and ask your pastor to sign up for that one as well.

3. Order video tapes of master preachers, teachers, and speakers. Your pastor can review them not so much for their content as for what they reveal about the style and methods by which top-rated speakers make themselves effective.

4. Many denominations offer video course material through their own continuing education offices, or by way of seminaries.

5. Regular college courses in public speaking are available in many communities, either as night school offerings or part of the daytime curriculum. Encourage your pastor to attend.

Q. We have some inactive members who say they aren't around because they "were not being fed spiritually. " How do I handle that?

A. The first thing you need to do is get them to talk further. What do they mean when they say they are not being fed spiritually? Listen for as many specifics as you can. Be careful not to lecture to them. As you listen to what they are not receiving, you will also be picking up valuable information about what they want to receive, what they need in order to feel nurtured spiritually.

You need extensive knowledge of the possible ways your church has available to feed people spiritually. Corporate worship is hopefully only one of the sources of spiritual growth. Talk about possibilities within your congregation. Koinonia groups, Bible study groups, prayer groups, and adult Sunday School classes are some examples. Be positive. Do not try to convince them that they, without realizing it, are actually being spiritually nurtured. Do not try to persuade them that the burden is theirs to take advantage of the plenty available in your congregation. Both efforts would be misguided and certainly fruitless.

People who feel spiritually hungry may in fact need an opportunity to discover, develop, and use their spiritual gifts. "Not being fed" may be an inaccurate diagnosis. That hunger may be instead an unrecognized need for more meaningful service, a need to experience what the priesthood of all believers is really about. Here's what one individual told me about a discovery a friend of hers made.

> My friend Janet said she always felt assurance in her relationship with God, but she missed the joy that the Bible talks about. She could never understand why. Then she became a Stephen Minister [a trained lay caregiver] in our congregation. She found joy. She found deep meaning when she began to minister and show love to people who have never realized before how much God loves them.

Now obviously an active member is not going to confront an inactive member with, "You are inactive because you have not yet found service that is meaningful to you." But your listening may enable the inactive member to discover it for him- or herself.

Appropriate avenues of service may not exist in your congregation, in which case perhaps you and the inactive member can develop one together. In such an instance, everyone wins: you, the inactive member, and the congregation. Thanks to the helpful feedback offered by the inactive member, a new avenue of service for more than just that individual may be opened up.

Q. We had a strong difference of opinion in our annual meeting about the budget. As a result, one member became inactive. When decisions of the congregation cause inactivity, what should we do?

A. People often believe that the proper approach in instances like this is to immediately discuss the decision or policy with the inactive member, arguing its merits and reasoning with the inactive member until he or she "understands." Many times argumentativeness is all that inactive members have received when they have disagreed with a particular decision or policy.

Push that all aside and just relate to the person. Perhaps it is surprising to you, but many times, with quality relating, the disagreement or policy difference subsides in importance. As you ask questions and listen, you may discover that the disagreement itself is secondary to other issues. The person may have felt rejection. He or she may have come to believe that "What I think or care about isn't important around here." Conflict of any kind may turn the person off, or perhaps church leadership handled the conflict poorly.

A good leadership technique for any possibly controversial subject is to use *anticipatory socialization.* That's a bit of managerial and human services jargon that simply means, "Tell people ahead of time what is likely to happen." Examine the consequences of church decisions and policy changes before they are made by talking about them in information exchange meetings, writing about them in letters and newsletter articles, and discussing them informally whenever possible.

Q. What about instances in which doctrinal or denominational practices conflict with a member's beliefs, causing him or her to become inactive?

A. First of all, differences about doctrinal or denominational practice are rarely the cause of inactivity. More often than not something else is going on, but the inactive member is using this explanation as a catch-all to stand for other issues. Through a caring and accepting relationship with the person, you stand a good chance of finding out what that "something else" might be.

If it develops that the individual is truly struggling greatly with a particular denominational practice, your care may enable the person to see that he or she can live with the situation. If that is not possible, then it might be well for the individual to find another church that more closely accords with the beliefs that he or she holds. In most instances you will be justified in calling this a victory rather than a defeat.

Note

1 Jack R. Gibb, "Defensive Communication," in *Messages: A Reader in Human Communication,* ed. Jean M. Civikly (New York: Random House, 1974), pp. 333-337.

12

Dealing with Hurt and Anger

Sometimes the feelings inactive members have are very personal, very deep. Sometimes what the inactive member is feeling is simply . . .

Hurt

Q. When a member has left the church because of hurt feelings, what is the best action to take?

A. Go to the individual, make personal contact, and listen. Get the person to talk about the hurt. After a time, you and the other may be able to assess how realistic the hurt feelings are. Many times the feelings will be a quite reasonable response to what happened; sometimes, though, the individual might have perceived hurt when none was intended.

If it is the perception of the individual, often just talking about the incident or issue with someone who obviously cares is enough. People mistakenly believe that caregiving in conflict situations means blame has to be assigned, the one who is at fault has to be identified. Frequently that's unnecessary. The fact of talking allows the individual to clear the feelings out

141

of his or her system and move on.

Avoid minimizing the hurt. Don't tell the other to forgive and forget, or to get over the feeling. Do not tell the individual he or she shouldn't feel that way. All these mistakes will do is make the other extremely resentful and angry. Instead of opening the door further to the truth, you have in effect asked the inactive member to lie to you the next time.

You may be able to bring together the inactive member and the individual (or the group) that was the source of the hurt. Better yet, with due caution, have the individual who caused the hurt make contact with the inactive member to apologize, or at least listen. Caution is in order because there is always the possibility of reopening wounds and renewing old disagreements rather than participating in a reconciliation.

Q. How long should listening to hurts go on? I spent 45 minutes in one visit listening to an inactive member describe her hurts, and it didn't seem to do any good at all.

A. What's the rush? You may not have given that person one-tenth of the time and care required. This question reflects a quick-fix mentality based on formulas rather than real people: I'll do this, then you do that, and everything's all better. Here is what one formerly inactive member said upon seeing this question:

> Someone who would say that must be kidding, or terribly unrealistic. In my case, when I was inactive, I lived with two years of hellacious experiences. My life was totally out of control. I felt like I could never again trust the world to be a safe and stable place. After that, 45 minutes is supposed to cure me and cast me back into the church as a victorious Christian? Be real.
>
> What I want active people to understand is that often we inactive members are not proud of feeling

the way we do. Under the bitterness is often a deep sense of shame and guilt that comes from a conviction we ought to be able to control ourselves better. We want your help, not your condemnation. We have plenty and enough self-condemnation. We need your caring concern to help free us from the prison of pain and shame we find ourselves in.

If you give up on us after a short visit, you have failed to see our problem in its complexity, and us in our need.

Q. How do you deal with an individual who absolutely refuses to come back to church or forgive those within the congregation who hurt him? This isn't just a case of his perceptions, either—the people he refuses to forgive really did hurt him.

A. Take a couple of steps backward and look at the whole situation and all the parties involved. Are you expecting some Herculean effort by the inactive member? Have you been telling this fellow he ought to ignore his feelings, or erase them, or what? Those are totally unrealistic demands. Human nature doesn't work that way. Here's the way a formerly inactive member puts it.

A lot of active church members think I'm exaggerating when I say that I was powerless to bring myself back to church. But it's true. Midway through my inactivity, I had come back, I had tried to stay, but I just couldn't even though I wanted to. I just couldn't. There were too many factors pushing me away from church.

Sometimes the case is that people get into a relationship with inactive members having certain expectations of them—maybe consciously, maybe not. The expectations go along these lines: This person is inactive, and that makes him (or her) a bad person. It is the bad person who should be required to make whatever adjustments are necessary, not the good people who are still in church.

The flaw here is that good and bad don't count in church, "since all have sinned and fall short of the glory of God" (Rom. 3:23), as the Apostle Paul writes the Christians at Rome, and us. "Good" Christians can do bad deeds whether in church or out.

A person who "absolutely refuses," as you put it, to return or forgive is often being rushed to forgive. But forgiving takes time. It's a process. The deeper the pain, the stronger the wrong, and the more sensitive the person, the longer the process will take.

Q. A member lost an election to a board he had been on for many years. He is hurt, and he and his wife no longer come to church. No amount of caring ministry works. What can we do?

A. Patiently and persistently keep the contact with the individual going. It's not really that "no amount of caring ministry works," but rather that *this amount* of caring ministry hasn't worked. Give the man time to work through his pain, and let caring persons be there to help.

From active members' standpoints, often, caring ministry has indeed occurred. But inactive members perceive the matter quite differently. What has often gone on in the name of "caring ministry" has been active members trying to talk inactive members into coming back to church, telling them they shouldn't feel hurt, perhaps sprinkling in a platitude or two, and icing it all with intimations about the inadequacy of the inactive members' faith. Plainly this is not caring ministry.

Another key point to remember is that causes of inactivity often come in clusters. There may be one precipitating event (the lost election in this instance), but that could be the last of a whole chain of circumstances creating stress in another's life. This fact explains why inactive members' strongly expressed feelings so often seem, to active members, out of proportion to the reason for inactivity first advanced by the inactive member. First on the inactive member's list to talk about will be the one precipitating event, but you will need to ask plenty of open-ended questions and do much more listening before you can be content that you really understand all the causes.

Anger

Q. I was visiting an inactive member, and I really got an earful. That person really let me have it with some strong feelings. What should I make of this? I am assuming there is relatively little hope.

A. On the contrary, when an inactive member lets loose with deep feelings, whether anger or something else, that is an extremely positive sign. Deep feelings mean deep care.

Q. How do I deal with feelings of hostility, anger, and resentment?

A. I know of only one way, and that is to let the inactive member get those feelings out. The more the person is able to vent those feelings, the better. You can play a crucial role by being a kind of sponge that soaks up those feelings as they spill over.

Avoid the temptation to argue with the individual. You might think you are called on to issue stern, moralistic warnings about forgiveness and "loving your brother." If your goal were to shut the inactive member up, this might work, but that's not your goal. Preachments like that would be the worst blunder you could make. Statements such as those do absolutely no good. Worse, they show you as insensitive and lacking understanding—you have not tried on the shoes of the inactive member. The greatest gift you can give the inactive member is your listening and acceptance of his or her feelings.

"But," some say, "I can't accept their feelings. I flatly disagree with the substance of their negative thinking. It would be dishonest of me to accept feelings like that." So often people think everything is a matter of being right or being wrong, and, "Since I am obviously right, then the other person has to be wrong. I have to make that person believe as I do, interpret the world as I see it."

What you can do is allow them to own their own opinion. People can have differences of opinion. You can say, "I respect your right to believe this way, but I happen to think differently." Let the inactive member be himself, be herself. I think that could be a real gift you can give someone. By listening patiently, you stand a good chance of participating in one of those beautiful moments with which God blesses us, when a person lets down barriers and lets you in to his or her innermost self.

Q. When inactive members are angry, and letting their anger out, are they more likely to be telling me the truth?

A. Yes, if you give them the chance. When inactive members are angry, that means they are still emotionally involved. If they're not angry (which happens after a passage of time), that's too bad because it means they probably aren't feeling any particular emotions about the church. That's when you worry.

Q. When the outburst is over, what should I say?

A. Thank the person. Say something like, "To show your anger like that is risky. Thank you for trusting me enough to share it, and thank you for the care you must still have for the church, to be that outspoken."

A formerly inactive member recalls the way she received a similar affirmation:

> The first time I ever shared the *whole story* of why
> I became inactive was some five years after I returned.
> After my sharing, the person I was talking to said,
> "Thank you for sharing that. You must be a very
> strong person to have been able to go through all of
> that." Wow, what affirmation and acceptance! That
> comment had curative power.

Q. What do you do for the member who has not attended
in years because of anger over an incident that happened 15
years ago? The entire church staff has changed since then. (He
is visited occasionally by the stewardship committee.)

A. First of all, keep the stewardship committee away from
him. It is obvious—and no surprise—that their visits have done
very little good. Having members of the stewardship committee
be the only people to visit an inactive member is probably worse
than having no one call on the person at all.

What you need to do is have another member of the congregation visit that person simply to find out how he or she is doing.
Just that. The incident that happened 15 years ago may come up,
if not in the first visit, almost certainly in a later one. That's not
surprising, either. While the congregation has moved on in the last
15 years, the inactive member has been locked in a time warp,
reliving the hurt and anger of that incident again and again. Only
someone's listening and then listening some more will allow the
inactive member to unlock these old perceptions and realities.

Don't try to gloss over the incident, don't try to explain it,
don't come down hard on the inactive member whatever you
do. Do apologize if it's appropriate, on behalf of the congregation. Then listen some more and leave the rest up to God.

Q. How do I gracefully handle a situation in which the
inactive member is rude and hostile?

A. As much as you can, wait it out. Respond with love and—internally!—with forgiveness. Very often when individuals have a chance to express their feelings in an accepting environment, feelings of hostility dissipate. The great majority of inactive members will not be rude and hostile, and many of those who appear to be are simply expressing their feelings of hurt and anger by lashing out at the nearest target, which happens to be you.

It's easier to absorb hostility when your own motivations are very clear in your mind. You may feel that the anger directed toward you is unfair, but if you are clear about your desire to help bring God's healing, you will see that the hostility of the other is a necessary step to move forward from anger. Then you won't take it personally.

The one exception to this recommendation for absorbing anger is if the other person is persistently and deliberately antagonistic. Church antagonists, as defined in Chapter 7, usually have a track record of destructiveness within the congregation or elsewhere. These individuals tend to be mentally disturbed, and no amount of love, compassion, or gentle absorption helps. Rather the opposite—such behavior feeds their hostility. It is extremely unfortunate, but with such individuals only firmness, strength, and sometimes an early good-bye are effective.

Other Relationship Situations

Q. How do I approach a person who is so busy with work and family (I think there are financial and emotional problems) that there seems to be no time for church? Is there some way to reach this person?

A. This is a situation that is screaming out for ministry. That person's inactivity may be the least of the problems in terms of immediate needs, immediate hurts. Once you have—or someone has!—offered support, you will be able to find out what this person's primary needs are. Church activity or inactivity will be low on the list, is my guess. Address those primary needs first. That is essential if the individual is ever even to consider coming back.

Q. What if someone has stopped attending because he or she has adopted a non-Christian faith—do I relate to that individual in the same way?

A. Initially your relating should follow the same course, that is, reach out and get in touch with the individual to find out what's going on in his or her life. Talk with the person, don't just write him or her off.

In the process of listening, the opportunity will arise for you to say, "Tell me about your new beliefs, your new faith. I'm interested in it." Learn from the person. Be Christ to him or her, and by that I don't mean to use the Gospel as a stick to beat the individual soundly about the head and shoulders, either. I mean be the personification of the love of Jesus Christ.

With people who claim to have totally changed their value system, don't be too quick to close the door. Here's what one individual shared with me:

> I've observed that people who get caught up in cults are often just pausing there, a stopping-off place for themselves. It fulfills an inner need for a time, but lacking the Gospel, there is still that unmet hunger to be in relationship with God through Christ, which ultimately resurfaces. Eventually many of these people move on to re-embrace the Christian faith fully. If we start with people where they are and simply love them, often the quality of our love can open the person to the reality of the greater love that is available from God.

Q. I visited an inactive member who said, "I can praise the Lord by myself at home." How should I have answered this person?

A. I don't think you need to answer the individual who says this. It doesn't look to me as if he or she is asking a question.

It is so easy to fall into the mode of thinking that whispers, "I have to rebut this person. I have to refute what this person says. I have to argue this person into good sense." No. It never works. What you have to do is listen to the individual. If someone says praising the Lord at home is possible, why argue? It's true, in part.

Of course, the issue is whether this is sufficient for the nurture of one's faith. But lecturing about that issue, however winsomely, will not serve Christ's cause or the inactive member's either.

Ask questions instead. How does the person praise the Lord at home? What are the strengths of this kind of praise? What are its weaknesses? Advantages? Drawbacks? Positive and negative aspects? Get them talking, and you be still. Don't ask these questions so you can build up a case against the individual, or in order to manipulate him or her into saying something you want said. Ask for information because you genuinely want it.

Again, I remind you, causes mostly come in clusters. During your listening you may unearth some very interesting points to talk further about.

Q. I called on a couple, parents of Sunday School children, who said, "Church is all right for children. But we don't need it ourselves." How should I relate to them?

A. I would start out by saying, "Tell me more. You've made an intriguing statement there, that church is all right for children but you don't need it. Fill me in." And then listen with every atom of your being.

Somewhere along the way you might ask, "What needs are being met for your children by church?" They'll have a response to that, no doubt. You could then ask, "Do you have any similar needs as adults?" They'll think about that. You might continue, "How are you getting those needs met at this time in your life?" And do be very careful not to come charging in with, "Ah-ha! You really do need the church, don't you!" Just leave the questions behind you as you go, and the echo of their own answers in their ears. You are hoping to make their brains itch a little, that's all.

While you're at it, look at your church from the perspective of this couple for a moment. What in fact is your church offering that is meat and potatoes for adults? Maybe a little soul-searching is in order. Maybe all that is available is pap— baby food. If so, you will have great cause to celebrate the perceptiveness of this couple and their gift to the church in sharing their observations.

Q. How can inactive members' legitimate reasons for not attending church be overcome?

A. Well, let's see. There's hypnotism. Brainwashing. Threats to break their kneecaps. . . .

I'm kidding, I hope. Too often, however, churches have adopted a winning-by-intimidation strategy. It doesn't work and it isn't Christian.

Anyway, why would anyone want to overcome an inactive member's *legitimate* reasons? What you want to do is find out what the person's needs are, and then see whether your church has the capacity to meet those needs.

You have your task, which is to hear the person out. If indeed the reasons they offer seem legitimate to you, "overcoming" them is not what you are called to do. You may be called to see what changes you can make in your congregation. You may be called to bless the person on his or her way. You may be called to wait for a while. You may be called to direct the person to a church that can fulfill needs your church cannot. Even so, periodically check in with the person to see what's going on, and whether there are ways your congregation can offer ministry.

13

To Invite or Not to Invite

At some point after you have developed a relationship with an inactive member, you will come to the moment when you wonder if now is the time to "pop the question" —to ask the inactive member to return to church. This chapter deals with what you ought to be considering in regard to that question. It also tells some important considerations for welcoming inactive members home when they do return.

Q. I've heard that even with our best efforts only a small fraction of inactive members will become active again. Is this true?

A. It's a lie. It's the devil's lie. The devil would love to have us think, "Why try? It won't make any difference anyway."

When congregations put forth their best effort, a very high proportion of inactive members will come back to church. What has been happening in the church, however, is that congregations have not been putting forth their best efforts, but their worst. Among other "worsts," they have been approaching the problem with a results orientation and a judgmental attitude.

Here's another way to look at that question, as a formerly inactive person remembers and responds:

> Do only a small fraction come back? Ask me. I came back. Ask Wendell, Rebecca, Evelyn, Robert, Cynthia, Gary, Janice, Frank, David, Debbie, Doris, Muriel, Lennie, Wayne, and Catherine, and on and on. I've known them all. Each of them is a unique human being in God's design, so full of life and love. Our congregation would be greatly diminished and deeply impoverished without their presence. I am so thankful they have returned home. They are family to us all.

Inactive members aren't proportions and statistics, but people with names. They are among the ones to whom Jesus was referring in his parable of the lost sheep:

> "And if he finds it, truly I tell you, he rejoices over it more than over the ninety-nine that never went astray. So it is not the will of your Father in heaven that one of these little ones should be lost."
>
> Matthew 18:13-14

Q. When do you give up on an inactive member?

A. Never.

Q. You mean there is never a time when I can expect to stop reaching out intentionally to establish contact and develop a relationship with an inactive member who doesn't return?

A. No, I don't mean that. When there is no relationship to hold on to, when no spark has been struck and no interest is evident, then you can back off. Even in this case, however, I might try again in six months. Your absence may result in a gap in the inactive member's life that he or she would welcome having filled again. Naturally you will put the person on your prayer list no matter what happens.

Q. How often do inactive members decide by themselves to return to church?

A. One hundred percent of the time. You delude yourself if you think you can make a decision for an inactive member, even in part. And that's the way it has to be because the inactive member has to be the one to own the decision. If he or she returns out of a misplaced desire to please you, or due to pressure of guilt or shame that you imposed, that inactive member will not be there long.

The best that you can do is create a loving and caring environment within which individuals are able to make decisions that are healthy and positive.

Q. How should I go about inviting an inactive member back to church?

A. The question is not *how,* but *when* and *whether.* In the context of a relationship, the how will pretty much take care of itself—if it's appropriate at all!

And there's the rub. In most instances, it is neither necessary nor appropriate to actually issue an invitation to return to church because the inactive member will do it for you. The inactive member will do the inviting if you wait patiently, listen caringly, and determine correctly what the person's needs are!

How can you be so certain that this will be the case? It is because your very presence, with the inactive member knowing full well that you are there out of concern and as a representative of the church, is all the invitation the inactive member will need.

You must wait because the inactive member's own mention of a desire to come back to church is the indicator that shows the individual is ready to consider it. By "jumping the gun" and issuing an invitation yourself, you run the strong risk of being premature. Issuing an invitation too late will not do much harm, if any. Issuing one too early may spoil the relationship you have developed.

Q. But what if the inactive member is a friend or a family member, someone who is not looking at me as even semi-officially or unofficially representing the church? Doesn't that person need an invitation?

A. You are correct, an already-existing close relationship is the exception to the rule. People who are never likely to see past your existing relationship will never put 2 and 2 together to make 4. They may never see your presence as an invitation.

Even in such instances, you need to wait until you have built up a certain trust level within the relationship. Don't make it the first topic you bring up, or even close! Long before you invite someone, you need to have prefaced your invitation with questions relating to the individual's feelings about God, about the church. Questions, not statements. Neither with perfect friends nor perfect strangers do you want to be caught telling them what they should feel, believe, or do, or bemoaning what they are not doing.

Q. Creating a favorable environment for an inactive member to want to return is one thing. But what about overcoming the inertia of inactivity—how do I help a person make that first move toward reinvolvement?

A. I heard a quote that seems applicable here:

> Don't try to climb a wall
>   that is leaning toward you;
> Don't try to kiss someone
>   who is leaning away from you.

If the person is leaning toward the church already, based on what he or she says, go ahead and invite. You don't have to keep climbing. If the person is leaning away from the church, or just standing still neutrally, don't invite. Just continue relating to the person in a caring way.

Here's an instance where an invitation was timed correctly, as reported by a formerly inactive member.

> The new pastor of our church had called on me, saying, "I heard you used to be very active at First Church, and I just thought I'd like to meet you." As we talked, I found myself sharing the skeleton of the story about why I was inactive. At the end, I said, "I'd like to come back, but, you know, this has just become a bad habit and I don't know how to get out of it."
>
> He answered with a very simple statement that has stuck with me: "If you want to come back, you have to start someplace. I'd like to invite you to come back this Sunday."
>
> Later, much later, I realized that the reason my pastor's invitation to return to church was so powerful and effective was because he didn't issue the invitation until he'd heard me out and I'd already said I wanted to go back. That's where the earlier contacts failed. They felt like pressure because the correct and reachable moment had not arrived for me.

I am initially cautious about giving a green light to working on someone's "inertia." Many times active members start a relationship off by trying to work on an inactive member's inertia, and that's just too quick. Care for and relate to the person, and wait until he or she says something first.

Having established these qualifiers, there are some possibilities for making the decision less threatening. When the time is right, and only then, you can suggest the person accompany you to a low-profile event rather than starting off with the main worship service. You could ask, "Will you come with me to hear this choral group next Sunday afternoon? They're supposed to be excellent." Or, as another example, you could say, "Would it be easier for you to 'get your feet wet' by going to the Saturday night service we've started offering during the summer months?" You could conceivably offer to do something besides church with the individual—go to a movie, out for dessert, or go bowling. This would deepen your relationship and make it natural for you to invite the person at a later time to accompany you to church.

Q. How do you handle objections to coming back to church?

A. You shouldn't have to handle many of these if you are holding off on the invitations and letting the inactive member do his or her own inviting. A relationship is not a chess game. This is not a case where an inactive member makes a move, you make a countering move, the inactive member makes a move, you make a countering move, and so on. People unknowledgeable in the area of caring for inactive members might think so. They might fantasize that as a result of their skill at counter-moves, eventually the inactive member will have been sufficiently reasoned with and will say, "I see. I have given you all my arguments for staying out of church, and you have countered them effectively. You win. I will come back to church and be very active."

Fantasy is what it is. Things don't work like that.

Q. So you're saying we can only love inactive members back into church?

A. No, I'm saying we can only love them.

Q. If I do relate caringly to inactive members as you suggest, is there some specific amount of time it takes for inactive members to feel free to return to church?

A. On an average the longer a person has been inactive, the greater number of contacts it will take for that person to decide to come back. This is a statistical assertion, but averages don't tell the story when you are dealing with a particular individual. Someone who has only briefly been inactive may take several visits or more; someone who has been inactive for two years might come back after only one visit.

Here's what one inactive member reports.

> I had been inactive for two years. It took 8 contacts of various forms (visits, happenstance encounters, and phone contacts), totaling about 4 hours to pave the way for me to come back.

This is the key point to remember: Issuing an invitation before the inactive member has spoken about wanting to come back to church will seem like pressure. After the person has stated a desire to return, however, a gentle non-pressure invitation at that point will seem like precious words of encouragement. An invitation then will carry great power for the inactive person. Both the words and the person who spoke them will be remembered.

Q. We had an every member visitation conducted by an outside organization. These people visited all our members, even inactives. (At their request, we identified who was active and who was inactive so that they could approach the inactive members differently.) In the course of their visits to inactives, there were many "I'm coming back" comments, yet few if any actually came back. What gives?

A. I suppose this must have been a stewardship drive, primarily. And maybe the inactive persons who said they were coming back were just being polite, without any real intention of returning.

But I think there's more to the story. Evidently there was

no follow-up with these inactive members after the outside organization packed up its bags and left. If my speculation is so, why would you expect the inactive members to come back? They made a gesture in that direction, which is more than should have been expected of them in the first place. But then no one followed through to establish a relationship with them.

How to Welcome Inactive Members Home

Q. There are those among our inactive members who would really like to come back to church, but they are afraid or embarrassed. How do I help people overcome their fear of rejection?

A. Spend time talking (actually, listening) to them about their fears. As you provide the reflective echo to what they are saying, they may be able to see which fears are realistic and which are not. Assure them, when it comes to their realistic fears—being stranded with no one to talk to, for example—that you plan to be available, to be with them.

Q. What are some of the fears inactive members have about reentry into the life of the church?

A. Your question is one that active members should be continually asking. It is a question that can result in greater empathy for inactive members.

Inactive members wonder . . .

- What will everyone think?
- Will I be accepted?
- Will people still consider me Christian?
- Will people recognize me?
- Will people make jokes at my expense?
- Was I missed?
- Will people look down on me now?
- Will anyone talk to me?
- Will people make too much fuss over me?

Probably in their worst fantasies, they imagine someone standing during the worship service to introduce them to the whole congregation: "Here's good old so-and-so, who hasn't been here for a while, but has seen the light at last."

Q. Is there some ceremony or ritual you would recommend to welcome inactive members back on their return?

A. Some denominations have specific rituals recommended or required when a member returns, a ceremony that is based on sound tradition. If this is the case with your denomination, go ahead and use it.

I have recently become acquainted with a Catholic rite, for instance, that involves a 12- to 18-month process of reconciliation and culminates with a joyous celebration and ritual in a worship service on Maundy Thursday. (Remember, reconciliation is a process that takes place on both sides of the fence.) This "re-membering" ritual is by and large reserved for Catholics who have been away from church for many years, sometimes decades. And there is no absolute requirement for any individual to participate.

If the liturgy or rite you might devise has as its chief outcome the humiliation or embarrassment of the inactive member—a sense of crawling back to the fold with one's tail tucked between the legs—then you're better off not doing it. You need to determine whether the ceremony builds up or tears down the returning inactive member. If the ritual of reconciliation is part of a process that affirms the person's standing in the community, in this earthly body of Christ, then the returning inactive member may very well see it as something he or she wants to be part of. You can also ask the returning inactive member what his or her feelings are about that. Embarrassment is what you want to avoid.

In general, assuming the individual has been inactive for a relatively brief time—perhaps months to one or two years— you would probably do well simply to welcome the individual back by private gestures, or perhaps by a more private ceremony in the pastor's office.

Q. How can we actively welcome those members returning after a relatively brief absence—no more than a year or two, say—without embarrassing them?

A. Generally, be friendly without being overly friendly. Don't blow the individual's return all out of proportion—don't make a big deal out of it. Envision yourself walking in the other person's shoes, and relate to them in the same way you would like to be related to. Here are some examples of appropriate statements to make:

- It's good to see you.
- How have you been?
- Can I get you a cup of coffee?
- How's your family?
- I'm happy to see you.

There are certain kinds of statements it is just as well not to say, too. Consider one very common—and usually very well-intended!—statement people make to a returning inactive member:

Active member: We've missed you.
Returning inactive member: If you really missed me so much, how come you didn't get in touch with me when I wasn't there? I don't believe you.

Most returning inactive members would be too gracious to say that in so many words, but there's a strong chance the thought would be there. What this imaginary dialogue reveals is how cheap the words *I missed you* or *we missed you* can seem to someone who was not sought out for weeks, months, or even years by the congregation. Even when you sincerely mean them, you need to be extremely careful in using these words.

Other examples of statements to avoid:

- Where have you been?
- Oh, you're back.
- It's about time you got your act together.
- Since you're back, let me sign you up for . . .

- Good grief, the roof's going to fall in!
- It must be Easter or Christmas if you're here.
- Are you new here? (Followed by guffaws)

If you really are uncertain whether an individual is new, say instead, "My name is _____. I don't believe we've met." That is an *I* message, not a *you* message. Notice how many of the objectionable statements are you messages.

Q. How do you get the church membership to be natural and not "say all the wrong things" when inactive members return?

A. Education and training—I know of no other way. There also ought to be exposure to some real folks who have returned, with the opportunity to get to know each other well. If you do that, people will develop an inner compass for sensing what direction is right when talking to an inactive member. So, I repeat, give the members of the congregation training and also give them person-to-person experience with those who have "been there" and returned.

Q. If an inactive member becomes active, what is the likelihood of inactivity happening again?

A. The likelihood of repeat inactivity is high if the congregation and individuals within the congregation are not addressing the original causes of the inactivity, to the extent that they have control over these causes and can help eliminate them. Moreover, if those same causes still exist, other members are also likely to become inactive. When a congregation is intentionally seeking to find out the needs of another, and then helping that person address those needs, the likelihood is lower.

Q. How do you convince reinvolved inactives that there is a need for their participation in church life?

A. First, be sure there are genuine needs. You have to be telling the truth about needs, and everything else. The needs should also be challenging. Newly active members—all members—want to be involved in more than just "slave labor." Administration and the other aspects of "keeping the church machinery going" are necessary, and they are right up the alley of some members. The Apostle Paul names *governance* as one of the gifts of the Spirit, in fact. But many members want to be involved in other activities involving more person-to-person type ministry.

One great gift that formerly inactive members bring to the church is the knowledge that their experience as inactive members gives them. They are often ideally suited, with training, to be part of a group that is charged with reaching out to inactive members.

Q. If people have been leaving because the church is experiencing excessive tension, do you work on the cause of tension or do you reach out to the people leaving?

A. This question is in a chapter about inviting people back, and welcoming them back, for one reason. It is very unproductive for someone to set about providing the best possible caring to an inactive member, becoming a bridge for the individual's return, only to have that individual return to an extremely inhospitable environment. What will the person do? Leave again, of course.

Hence the answer is both. You must reach out to the inactive member who is hurting because of the strife in the congregation, but you had certainly better apply every resource available to the task of getting that strife eliminated.

14

Discipline and Other Difficult Decisions

When you are genuinely intent on finding out the needs of inactive members, the time may come when you are faced with some tough questions that require difficult decisions. The first difficult area to deal with is the area of discipline—for some denominations this involves deciding whether people should be removed from the membership rolls.

Termination and Transfer

Q. Is there a time when we should drop an inactive member from the membership list?

A. Yes, there is such a time. It is when the inactive member says that he or she absolutely does not want to be a member of the congregation. There is no call for congregations and active members to keep banging their heads against a wall of indifference and frustration. Neither is there any call to keep harassing an inactive member who says in no uncertain terms that he or she wants to be left alone.

Congregations and denominations sometimes have rules, too, that define whether or not a member is inactive. Even where there are no bylaws or rules as such, congregations have membership lists to help members be accountable to one another. But if a member clearly states he or she wants no such accountability, or accepts no such accountability, then it would be inconsistent to maintain that person on the membership list. The key is to be careful not to write someone off prematurely, which would be irresponsible and even cruel.

Q. Some of the leaders in my congregation have been heard to say, "Those people are an expensive luxury for us," referring to inactive members. They are thinking about the denominational assessment based on membership, and of the cost of mailings and so on. The position of these leaders is that we ought to "get rid of the deadwood," clean up our membership list to reflect only active members. How can this attitude be countered?

A. What you are asking about here has to do with the motivation for removing someone from the membership list. Personally, I think to make money the guiding principle is shortsighted at best, sinful at worst. I hasten to qualify that statement, however, by declaring that I do know there are some congregations that are in financial difficulty, and that this issue is bound to come up as one partial solution to their troubles.

As a solution, I think "cleaning the rolls" is an illusion. It begins a process of paring that may not be complete until the membership roster is empty altogether. Such a congregation would be better-advised to begin real ministry to their inactive members. As reasons for inactivity become apparent, and needs are addressed, the church may find—is highly likely to find— that its decline in vitality is arrested and reversed.

When financial considerations become a significant factor in keeping or removing names from the membership list, it is a sure sign of many years of congregational neglect of inactive members. Each year a few more have become inactive and nothing has been done as the needs for ministry became more and more acute. Then, all of a sudden, when the total cost gets above some acceptable level, the first solution to be proposed is to write the individuals off. "Forget 'em. Out of sight, out of mind."

Sorry, it's not according to the grace we preach and teach. I sympathize with the plight of financially strapped churches, but suggest the need to look elsewhere for solutions. I also challenge these congregations to perform quality ministry with inactive members.

Q. An inactive member is attending worship services elsewhere, but he is very resistant to the idea of transferring his membership. He wants to continue his membership in our church. What should we do?

A. Sit down with that member and find out why he wants to continue membership. Until you have heard the person out, you can't make a loving decision. Try to resolve the situation, but do not let it continue indefinitely.

Q. What should bylaws say about terminating inactive members, keeping in mind that we are to love one another as Christ loved us? I realize you don't want to tell any church how to write its bylaws, but if you were starting a church from scratch, what would you want the bylaws to say?

A. I would make sure there was a caring, communicating process built into the bylaws. I would make sure that no favorites were played—that the same process applied to one and all. I would not allow financial status, whether of the church or the inactive member, to be the deciding factor. If, after the congregation had reached out in true compassion, the inactive member had clearly stated a wish to be removed from the membership list, then I would honor that request.

You know enough about what I mean by *true compassion* by this time to know that I don't mean one perfunctory telephone call or visit and that's it. I mean just what you mean:

Loving one another as Christ loved us. I don't think I can place a time limit for true caring—it could be a month, it could be a year. Looking for biblical guidance, I return to Luke 13:6-9 in which the gardener pleaded for an additional year *after* the land-owner had determined to cut the tree down. That seems like a pretty good standard to follow.

Q. If someone asks to be removed from the roster of the congregation, do we just simply do this, or do we pursue them?

A. When someone asks to be removed, call the person on the telephone and say something like:

> "We've just received your letter requesting that you be taken off the membership rolls of the congregation. I appreciate your getting with us on this. So often people leave a church without saying anything, they just disappear and we never hear from them. So I really appreciate your contacting us."

Then, depending on the situation, I might make a connection with the relationship the congregation has had with this individual or family:

> "We've certainly gone through a lot together. I remember your kids in Sunday School, and I remember you in that class we had. You've been members here for a good while."

These are only examples. You are looking to express the connection between you that gives you the right to ask what you want to ask, namely, for a chance to sit down together so you can learn how your congregation can better its ministry to all its members. The final part of the phone conversation might go something like this:

> "I would certainly enjoy sitting down with you and talking about what's going on with you, what your thoughts are. I'd like to find out what we did right and what we might have done wrong. Maybe we ought

to be celebrating with you, maybe we even owe you an apology, I don't know. I'm sure of this, though—we could probably learn a lot about how to make our ministry more effective. Would you agree to meet with me? I can promise this: My purpose is not at all to try and talk you into reconsidering your decision."

Sometimes individuals will go along with this request, sometimes not. It certainly doesn't hurt to try, and it can be a valuable opportunity for you to learn. Don't make the mistake of trying to force a reconsideration of the person's decision once you get there. Go for the purpose of a loving, caring exit visit, and that's all.

Q. If we do decide to take someone off the membership roll, what is the best way to go about it?

A. Have a personal visit with the individual, as suggested in the preceding answer, if he or she will agree. Thank the person for choosing to affiliate with your congregation in the first place. Wish the person well. Offer yourself personally or the congregation as a spiritual resource center if the individual wants to avail him- or herself of it. Offer a blessing if you are comfortable doing so.

By the way, just because the person is no longer on the membership list does not mean that you should have no more contact. Keep the lines of communication open, if possible. And by all means keep the individual on your permanent prayer list.

Don't drop someone from the membership roll by letter alone. You will further hurt the inactive member, and you may hinder that individual's building of a relationship with another—or your—congregation at some point in the future.

Q. What would you suggest be done about people who are still on the membership list but have moved out of town?

A. There is still an opportunity for ministry by your congregation with respect to individuals who have moved. You are still their church home until they choose to transfer membership or otherwise notify you of their intentions.

One choice, not necessarily the best one, is to send a letter. Here is a sample letter I've seen that I like the feel of.

> Dear _____,
>
> We have been thinking of you recently. We wonder if you've found a church home in your new community. If so, we would appreciate knowing the name and address of the church so we can officially transfer your membership.
>
> If you are still choosing your new church home, may we suggest the following church(es) in your area:
>
> If in the future you return to our area, either temporarily or permanently, please join us for worship. We would enjoy renewing our ties with you.
>
> May God richly bless you.
>
> In Christ,
(signed)

As I said, however, I don't think a letter is the best way to proceed. First I recommend calling the individual and asking how he or she is doing in the new community. Then you might say, "Since you have moved, we wanted to check with you to see what you would like to do about your membership." Then let the person talk. If the individual mentions being involved in another congregation, ask about it. Be interested—I assume you would be. If there is no mention of another church, offer to arrange for a congregation in the person's area to get in touch. If the person declines your offer, respect his or her wishes. If the person accepts, be sure you follow through fairly quickly.

I believe all church experiences ought to be as warm and positive as we can make them. Letters, even when written with the best of good will, are more impersonal than phone conversations. The individual's relations with the church are worth the few dollars a phone call costs.

Q. When a person is taken off the church rolls because of inactivity, and at the individual's request, should that person have to join again as a new member if and when he or she ever decides to return?

A. The rules or procedures of your denomination may be the guiding factor here. If no established policy exists, then do what is least embarrassing to the individual. Re-engage the person with the congregation with as little fanfare as possible, simply as a matter of being as caring as possible. Certainly recognize the person's return, and rejoice. But try to avoid embarrassment.

Q. Should our main concern be to bring an inactive person back to our church, or to encourage the individual to find a Christian church somewhere?

A. Neither of these alternatives is the main concern for you in caring for inactive members. Rather, your main concern is find out what that person's needs are so that you can minister to those needs. You don't have the power in any case to "bring them back" or "send them elsewhere."

Q. If an inactive member is not going to have needs met in my congregation, how do I direct that individual to another congregation?

A. Be sure that your assumption is true, first. Many times it merely sounds like the individual's needs can't be met in your congregation, but after sufficient careful listening you will find that there are other factors involved. Then add to that the fact that listening alone may be enough to dissipate the inactive individual's concerns. Sometimes, however, redirection is called for when an individual's needs for whatever reason cannot be met by your congregation. This is not often going to be the case, but when it is you should learn to do it without judgment or guilt.

Q. Can you foresee a situation in which a person has grown spiritually, and therefore needs to "graduate" from one congregation to another?

A. I think you can look at this more as a matter of gifts than graduation. The idea of graduating has a certain superiority built into it that is inappropriate. An individual may change, however, or may discover gifts for which there are no outlets in the present congregation. Sometimes one person's beliefs or gifts just may not fit, and then it may be necessary for him or her to move on. I would hope, though, that congregations would make an earnest effort to be aware of this possibility all the time, and would continually work to create new outlets for people.

"Paper Tiger" Difficulties

Sometimes, as in the questions that follow, the decisions that congregations have to make only seem tough. They are "paper tigers."

Q. I've heard statistics that suggest it takes ten times more effort to reactivate an inactive member than to bring in a new member. If that's so, why don't we just forget about inactive members and concentrate on bringing in new members?

A. An analogy occurred to me as I was listening to your question. Suppose someone asked me this:

> "Our teenage daughter just ran away from home. We know it will be a lot of trouble to try to reach out to her. My wife and I are still quite healthy, and

pregnancies for my wife have not been difficult. We were wondering if you think it would be a better expenditure of our time and effort to just forget about our runaway daughter and have another child. What's your advice?"

What do you think I would say to a question like that?

Getting back to your question, it has the same moral overtones as the choice offered to Sophie in the movie *Sophie's Choice.* A concentration camp guard told Sophie one of her children had to die, but she could pick which of the two it would be. Implicit in your question is the same kind of choice: Which of God's children should live, and which should die?

I have heard the parable of the sower used in support of this notion—as if to say that all we are responsible for is casting the seed, and then the poor Christian plants must struggle as best they can to survive. Those "lucky enough," blessed enough to be in good soil will thrive; everyone else is down the tubes. That is a misunderstanding of the teaching. It is not that active Christians are *in* the good soil; active Christians *are* the good soil. That fact makes this parable a very good one in support of preventive efforts. In effect, part of prevention becomes building up the quality of the soil.

I remember another parable from Luke 13:6-9 in which the gardener pleads that a fig tree be spared until he has had a chance to cultivate and fertilize it. Inactive members have been welcomed into the membership. We therefore have a responsibility to care for them as members of the family, not dismiss them as intractable statistics. Christ wants the lost to be found (Luke 19:10)!

I do not agree that it necessarily takes ten times more effort to reactivate an inactive member than to bring in a new member. This may be true only with respect to inactive members who have been gone a very long time. And even in these instances, let's not forget that the Gospel is God's explosive power unto salvation (Romans 1:16). As you become more aware and sensitive as an individual, and as your congregation likewise becomes more aware and sensitive to the needs of people, you will be reaching out to inactive members sooner. Relationships in such instances will be much easier to establish.

Finally, there is the rich resource that inactive members represent. They are people with many talents and gifts, often to become among the strongest of the supporters of the church's work in mission and ministry. They are exciting to know and develop a relationship with. The questions they are asking and the needs they are expressing may be precisely what a congregation needs to grow in its own spiritual dimensions as it responds to the challenges inactive members raise.

Q. How do we balance the time spent "reclaiming" inactive members and prevention of inactivity, on the one hand, with the needs of active members on the other? Long-term active members may start to feel like the older brother in the prodigal son story.

A. Especially when it comes to prevention of inactivity, as you will learn in the next chapter, no balance is required because the needs you are addressing are the needs of all—that's what makes it prevention in the first place. The congregation will be stronger and better overall. Benefits will flow to all.

The emphasis in caring for inactive members is on their *membership.* These are not "people from away," as Vermonters express it. They are members of the family. The relationship is even more intimate than that, according to St. Paul: They are part and parcel of the same body!

Mostly this is an unfounded fear in any case. I have yet to run into a congregation where so much time and effort is devoted to inactive members that active members feel slighted.

Q. The inactive member I have been visiting doesn't want to come back to church, but he is open to my continued visitation. Is there ever a time when I would decide I should stop visiting him?

A. This is a frequently asked question, and it is also a mostly theoretical question. I have never seen a situation where someone has been relating well with an inactive member, and it just went on and on, with no change, no growth taking place. This is not a prescription for burdensome duty, either. Somewhere along the line, if it hasn't happened already, you are going to develop a friendship with that person. Sometime along the way there will certainly be opportunity to discuss faith and share the Gospel. Spending time with a friend and talking about matters of highest importance is not a burden but a delight.

Basically, the answer to this question is: As long as the person needs the care and the love that you have to offer, continue to offer it. The real-life situations you will encounter will make the significance of this question pale. When you meet real people with real names and real needs, the thought of "leaving them to their fate" will not enter your mind.

15

More than an Ounce of Prevention

Your own experience with inactive members and your exposure to the sadness and seriousness of the causes of inactivity have prepared you for this chapter on prevention. A congregation that is working with deliberate intent to prevent inactivity is one that is saving itself and its people a lot of grief.

This same congregation is doing more, though. It is also creating for itself an environment in which mission and ministry can flourish. Prevention is not a series of negative, forestalling moves, but a positive building up of the church to be God's home—a place within which the world marvels, "See how they love one another."

Look first at some questions about . . .

Prevention in General

Q. What are the best ways to prevent inactivity?

A. There are as many ways to prevent inactivity as there are ways to create wholesome, homelike, healthy environments. Here are five of the most powerful:

1. Emphasize quality worship.

For me, *quality worship* is an experience that leaves the worshippers feeling closer to God and challenges them for ministry. For a friend of mine the phrase means "worship that passes the goose bump test." For you it perhaps means something else because there is a great variety of tradition within the Christian church. This is the way one pastor of a small community church in Massachusetts put it:

> There should be an atmosphere of community, a sense of unity of purpose in worshipping God where the people come with the expectation that they will be in the presence of God and leave with certainty that God has delighted in their presence.

In Christian worship the message of the Gospel in all its "for-you-ness" should come through, and the service should be conducted "decently and in order" (1 Cor. 14:40), as St. Paul says.

2. Foster meaningful relationships.

There ought to be social opportunities—times for fun—in plenty. There also ought to be small groups, both task-oriented and relationship-oriented. Most churches have plenty of the task-oriented kind of groups, but are short on relational small groups. Remember that bonding and a sense of continued importance are both important parts of why members stay active. If members have significant relationships within the church, they are far less likely to become inactive.

3. Assess needs of the congregation continually.

Be interested in the needs of every member, and take steps to find out what those needs are. Ask—by means of surveys, visits, informal conversations—each person what his or her needs are. Then tailor programming and services in your congregation to those discovered needs.

Asking once is not enough. There are always new people within a congregation who need to be listened to. There are changes in people's lives and changes in the circumstances of the church that raise new needs.

4. Provide open channels of communication.

People need a convenient and healthy way to share feelings—this is one aspect of open communication. If frustrations and hurts can be aired within the context of a listening, caring congregation, for example, there is much less reason for people to remove themselves from that context by becoming inactive.

5. Equip people for ministry.

Education and training of as many as possible in the congregation for real ministry is another way to prevent inactivity. When the priesthood of all believers is made a reality in people's lives, it is relatively much more difficult for them to entertain the notion of becoming inactive. Individuals whose discipleship has been enabled gain a reason for existence that only the church provides.

Q. I'm getting the idea that if we take prevention seriously, our congregation may have to make some changes. Any suggestions on how to make this medicine go down smoothly?

A. You're right. Inactivity is often a systemic issue. Congregations may need to change those systems they have in operation that work fine for most members, but to the detriment of some.

Your question shows you to be properly respectful of the trauma that changes can cause. Nobody minds requiring somebody else to change. It's when the necessity of change strikes close to home—well, that's different. We are just fine, thank you. No changes necessary here.

Consider that a bit with me.

People come to church for many different reasons, with a unique set of needs for each unique person. No one gets all his or her needs met by church, but it's reasonable to expect that at least some needs will be met by a congregation. If this doesn't happen, people often—and perhaps understandably—become inactive.

Much of what there is to say about prevention of inactivity relates to unfulfilled needs. "Unfulfilled Needs" is an omnibus cause of inactivity that encompasses many causes. You understand, I am sure, that I am not talking about frivolous needs, or unrealistic ones: Individuals who believe that the pastor can and should spend three hours every week with them in casual conversation; people who feel they should be in charge of every activity; or people who think that every Sunday worship service should be as polished as the productions they have seen put on by some televangelists.

Take care as you consider what might need changing to prevent church inactivity in your own congregation. Treat everyone's feelings and concerns with respect. People resist change by nature. Making changes is a drawn-out and sometimes arduous process.

Q. What kind of needs do you mean? What kind of needs might be going unmet that we should be trying to fill?

A. To answer that question, you need to look at the kinds of expectations people bring with them to church. Some (probably most) expect the church to provide for their spiritual needs, to help them make sense out of a confusing world; others are hoping for companions in their walk with Christ. At times people have emotional needs that the church has traditionally tried to meet, especially in times of crisis. Some hope the church will be the place where they can form meaningful relationships.

The kind of changes that a congregation might make would have nothing to do with changing the core, with changing the sum and substance of a congregation's beliefs. You need to be true to who you are. You certainly can be, without making that a license to be narrow or narrow-minded in your mission and ministry.

The best way to find out the needs in your congregation is to ask. Ask everyone—active members and inactive members alike. Then listen. Then listen some more. And finally, take action. Make those changes you are able to make.

Q. We don't have a lot of inactive members, as we are a fast-growing church. (We've gone from 200 members to 600 in four years.) My question is, how can we prevent members from becoming inactive as the growth process continues?

A. You probably have more inactive members than you realize, but are just not noticing them. Often when many new members are being added, the departure of others through the back door is not noted.

Obviously you are doing something right, and your expressed concern suggests what that is—loving care for each member of the flock. Keep that concern. Of the many points I mentioned in the preceding answer, the ones that you are most likely to be doing well now are those connected with worship and meaningful relationships. As the congregation grows, pay special attention to needs assessment and open channels of communication. Large churches have to be quite deliberate about setting up smaller groups, because it is within these that people can be heard most readily.

Prevention in Particular

Q. How do we change the perception of the church as a place that only contacts individuals in order to ask for money?

A. The key to changing this is in actions, not words. I remember in high school, when I was in our church youth group and heard that the congregation was going to make an "every-member-visitation," I thought, what a great idea! Everyone will have a visitor coming for no other reason than that the congregation cares. I also remember how crestfallen I was when our youth group director responded to my pleased excitement by saying, "Well, Ken, yes and no. The every-member-visitation is actually just a name for our stewardship drive."

Wouldn't it be nice for churches to schedule an every-member-visitation that was just that? An exploration with all members of how they are doing in their walk with Jesus Christ—that would be fantastic! I'm not putting down the church's need for money, but I think the perception you mentioned is based on fact—that too often money is the only reason churches contact their members. And the way to change the perception is to change the facts.

Q. Would it help prevent inactivity if our church required each new member to make some discipleship commitment at the time of joining? Would this be an encouragement to servanthood, or would it lead to mindless following?

A. I do believe people should be challenged to meaningful involvement when they join a congregation. When people join congregations they typically have a degree of enthusiasm that is waiting to be captivated by real, practical involvement. Churches that don't have programs or capabilities for steering this energy shouldn't be too surprised if many of their members drift toward inactivity.

Church life is basically a volunteer offering, so requiring commitments can get a little sticky. If the church itself is committed to helping members discover their gifts, and then to being a channeling source for them to employ these gifts, that's a positive outlook. On the other hand, if the church sees its members as all needing to move in lockstep, all equally committed to all aspects of the church's mission and ministry, that is a denial of the validity of individual gifts.

Q. What is the best way to get newcomers active in the programs of the church without their feeling pushed too much?

A. You can greatly reduce the likelihood of individuals feeling pushed if you simply ask them what their needs and preferences are. It is amazing how seldom people are asked, and how glad they are to answer when they are asked. Find out what people want to do, what excites them, where they would really like to minister. Then equip them for the task and stand out of the way!

Q. Since you have so consistently stated that meeting people's needs is a major way to prevent inactivity, what would you say to a congregation's periodically checking with its members about their needs and the best way to meet those needs?

A. I'd say: "I think it's a fantastic idea!" And don't stop there—of what you discover, implement what you can.

Q. What can we do to make church more meaningful?

A. Church is the place—the only place, to my knowledge—where people are challenged to do the impossible and then given the strength, grace, and enablement to work at it. Your congregation must be that place too. One active church member described it like this.

> What's made church more meaningful for me is getting into serving in ways that challenge me through and through. I am taking risks at the level where the only way I could possibly succeed is if God were with me, empowering me, letting him work through me. I'm doing things that would be impossible for me in my own strength, but God's grace makes them possible. Church is never boring to me, no church work is lacking in meaning because such a level of living and serving is daily exciting.

Q. How do you minimize the number of post-confirmation young people who virtually disappear?

A. Many is the earnest author who has pondered that question in many an earnest book. Because youth is such a time of upheaval, probably not all youth inactivity can be prevented. Still, some can be. Here are some suggestions:

1. **Ask youth what their needs are. Then listen, listen, listen to what they say.**

   The church has often designed ministry and programming for youth based on what adults think they need, or even on what adults think they ought to need, which will be even further off target. The listening and asking that ought to be done should take place before young people hit that dangerous post-confirmation age.

2. **Design ministry and programming that really meet the needs of youth.**

   Once you have discovered what youth say they need, provide it. This is not going to mean a lot of fancy, frivolous, or expensive activities, either. Young people are looking for satisfaction of a number of "bread-and-butter" spiritual needs.

3. **Invest in youth programming and ministry.**

   Churches get back what they put in to youth programming or any other endeavor. What amount is listed in your congregation's budget for "youth ministry"? Time and time again I have seen budgets where the amount listed was $200, $250, or $300—some pittance to show good faith on the part of the church, presumably. Many of those same congregations are the very ones bemoaning the poor functioning of their youth ministry. What such a picayune investment really shows is how low on the totem pole youth ministry is.

   In many ways the needs of youth as inactive members are no different from anyone else's needs. Therefore, you treat them with respect as fellow-redeemed who possess an abundance of grace. Youth are testing parental and church values, and biblical standards. Listen to them and love them. These are crucial years. How the church treats youth now will affect their perception of the church in later years.

Q. I've heard it said that some people join a large congregation for the sake of anonymity. Do you have any comments about the truth of this? If it is true, what can a congregation do about it?

A. I think it sometimes is true, but I don't think it's worth punishing anyone for. I seriously doubt that anyone expects total invisibility. My informed guess is that some people are just looking for lowered exposure. There are many aspects of people's lives that can make lowered exposure a desirable goal. They may be living very full and very busy lives, or have serious concerns that are taking all their energy.

Basically my reaction to this concern is take it easy. Don't whip yourself into a frenzy about these people. Nurture them, get to know them, find out what they need without prejudging them. Do good quality ministry. Offer programs that make your congregation an "attractive nuisance" to the people who are minimally active. What do I mean by *attractive nuisance?* Make your congregation's offerings so desirable that they insinuate themselves into the awareness of those persons who are determined not to get involved.

Q. In churches I've been part of, people think they're very committed if they come to worship two out of every four Sundays. Is this a mentality the church just has to live with?

A. You've been around my answers enough at this point to know that I wouldn't want you lowering the boom on anyone, whatever their attendance pattern. You may want to schedule a visit to check in with the person, find out what's going on, what needs the individual has.

Another approach you can take is to make sure your church is offering the very best worship experiences in its reach, the very best programming possible. One such worship experience or one particularly apt educational offering might be the one that makes people rise to the challenge for greater involvement that God is always offering.

Here's what one individual reported:

> In my part of the country, where 70% of the residents aren't involved in church at all, we would consider someone who attends two Sundays out of four as an active member. If that represents a change in pattern for the individual, however, we would probably get in touch with the person to learn what we could.

Q. How might the principles and training you suggest for caring for inactive members apply to evangelizing? I wonder if the same ideas might not be workable when I am calling on new-member prospects.

A. You are correct, there are many similarities. There are also some differences.

One of the differences is that with new members you will have had no previous contact, no previous attachment. With inactive members you start from the common base that both they and you have an attachment to the church. Even where you do not know the inactive member personally, still you both have in common the experience of your church.

Another difference has to do with inviting. With new members, you may be very explicit about inviting them to your church. With inactive members, you will wait until they themselves have brought up the subject of their possible return.

With an inactive member the chances are there is some hurt or brokenness that needs to be cared for over a fair period of time. New member prospects may of course be another church's inactive members, and hence need the same kind of care. If so, you will discover that by listening. Ordinarily, though, they will be new to your area, or not connected to any church at all. There will often be a built-in positive view of your church with new members, more of a mixed view with most inactive members.

16

A Vision for You and Your Church

One question I have not previously treated you to is this one: What Scripture verses would you recommend we share with inactive members? And the reason is very simple—I can't think of any that would be appropriate to share with inactive members *if the purpose were merely to cast a light of judgment on their inactivity.* There are those who wish I were more ready to do that. Perhaps they imagine that Jesus, when he dined with tax collectors and assorted sinners, spent his time haranguing them about their sinfulness. It is true that Jesus did some haranguing, but it was hard-hearted, self-justifying active members of the church that he singled out for the brunt of it.

No, I won't add any fuel to the judgment fires.

I can, however, think of a number of verses that you can keep in mind for yourself. These are Scripture verses for your encouragement, your edification, your support in this vital work. They are verses that speak to what attitude you can hope for, and what strength and enablements will be yours as gifts from God. Taken collectively, they are a vision of the work, a vision for your church, and a vision for you from the perspective of the throne of God.

> "Whoever welcomes you welcomes me, and whoever welcomes me welcomes the one who sent me."
>
> Matthew 10:40

In this passage Jesus reminds you of whom you represent when you knock on the door of the inactive member. You are the presence of Christ.

> "And whoever gives even a cup of cold water to one of these little ones in the name of a disciple—truly I tell you, none of these will lose their reward."
>
> Matthew 10:42

You are there to be the living water of Christ by your presence with the inactive member. You are there not to punish, but to refresh someone who is almost surely thirsty.

> "What do you think? If a shepherd has a hundred sheep, and one of them has gone astray, does he not leave the ninety-nine on the mountains and go in search of the one that went astray? And if he finds it, truly I tell you, he rejoices over it more than over the ninety-nine that never went astray. So it is not the will of your Father in heaven that one of these little ones should be lost."
>
> Matthew 18:12-14

Though this passage can refer to those not saved, it is a crucial one to set the tone for any congregation's rationale for being concerned for inactive members.

> "Again, truly I tell you, if two of you on earth agree about anything you ask, it will be done for you by my Father in heaven. For where two or three are gathered in my name, I am there among them."
>
> Matthew 18:19-20

Jesus reaffirms the power you come equipped with when you visit inactive members, and covenants to be with you in the caring you offer.

> "The greatest among you will be your servant. All who exalt themselves will be humbled, and all who humble themselves will be exalted."
>
> Matthew 23:11-12

In this passage Jesus sounds the call to servanthood and explains it in the same breath. You go to the inactive member not as superior to inferior, not even as equal to equal, but as servant.

> "And the king will answer them, 'Truly I tell you, just as you did it to one of the least of these who are members of my family, you did it to me.'"
>
> Matthew 25:40

And this is why your servant status makes sense—because when you serve, you are serving Christ in the person to whom you are reaching out.

> Rejoice with those who rejoice, weep with those who weep.
>
> Romans 12:15

The Apostle Paul speaks to the kind of empathy and compassion you are to show to the inactive member.

> Therefore, my beloved, be steadfast, immovable, always excelling in the work of the Lord, because you know that in the Lord your labor is not in vain.
>
> 1 Corinthians 15:58

And Paul suggests what kind of results you can expect when you leave results to God. Your labors will not be in vain.

> Face plain facts. Anybody who is convinced that he belongs to Christ must go on to reflect that we all belong to Christ no less than he does.
>
> 2 Corinthians 10:7 (Jerusalem Bible)[1]

When you are tempted to assume that your faith must be stronger than the inactive member's faith, Paul's words should give you pause.

> Bear one another's burdens, and in this way you will fulfill the law of Christ.
>
> Galatians 6:2

You are to join with the inactive member in sharing the load of hurt he or she may be carrying because Christ's law of love commands you to it.

> So let us not grow weary in doing what is right, for we will reap at harvest-time, if we do not give up. So then, whenever we have an opportunity, let us work for the good of all, and especially for those of the family of faith.
>
> Galatians 6:9-10

These words of the Apostle Paul can spur you on to perseverance in your care for inactive members, who are still part of the family of faith.

> Do nothing from selfish ambition or conceit, but in humility regard others as better than yourselves. Let each of you look not to your own interests, but to the interests of others.
>
> Philippians 2:3-4

This call to humility precedes that wonderful passage in Philippians in which Paul describes the humility of Christ in making himself a servant of all humanity.

> Be tactful with those who are not Christians and be sure you make the best use of your time with them. Talk to them agreeably and with a flavor of wit, and try to fit your answers to the needs of each one.
>
> Colossians 4:5-6 (Jerusalem Bible)[2]

Though this passage specifically refers to the way to talk to outsiders, it is also ideal in its description of how you should talk to inactive members. Note the emphasis on discovering needs.

> So deeply do we care for you that we are determined

to share with you not only the gospel of God but also our own selves, because you have become very dear to us.

1 Thessalonians 2:8

It is my earnest hope that this passage would describe to a "T" the nature of the relationships you form with inactive members.

Therefore encourage one another and build up each other, just as indeed you are doing.

1 Thessalonians 5:11

This is another description of the nature of the relationship you and the inactive member can form.

Always be prepared to give an answer to everyone who asks you to give the reason for the hope that you have. But do this with gentleness and respect. . . .

1 Peter 3:15b (NIV)[3]

Your opportunity to share Scripture, your faith, your feelings about church and worship and God, all come when and if the inactive member asks you to "give the reason for the hope that you have." Other than this, you are to rely on God to work his work in the inactive member's heart. You may be certain the inactive member will not be left alone by God, nor will you be.

These passages from Scripture are but a small sampling of the great riches in the Bible relating to inactivity and Christian relationships. Others may spring to mind for you. As you and I have passed through the trial of answering the tough questions regarding church inactivity, sometimes I have alluded to still other passages that would be instructive for you to study. For now, though, examine the ones highlighted for you here. Absorb them as part of the attitude and strength you must have to be the best caring person you can be.

No question and answer book that deals with the richness of human relations can ever hope to cover a subject so infinitely varied in its detail. These questions and my answers launch you along the way, I trust, with more confidence that you know at least some of what to expect.

The vision I lift up for your church, and for the Church at large, too, is a vision of the church as God's home, where the love of Christ is shared abundantly. And if God's home, then your home, and a home for all the members, for he has invited us in as members of his family that our joy may be complete.

Now I wish you well on your journey of learning and growth. From here on you will be doing, and your learning will increase in leaps and bounds, as suggested by the old Chinese proverb:

> I hear and I forget.
> I see and I remember.
> I do and I understand.

God be with you in your doing, and may the love of our Lord Jesus Christ sustain you in his work.

Notes

1 *The Jerusalem Bible,* ed. Alexander Jones (Garden City, NY: Doubleday, 1966).

2 *The Jerusalem Bible.*

3 *The Holy Bible, New International Version* (New York: International Bible Society, 1978).